JAMES I

JAMES I

Frank Dwyer

CHELSEA HOUSE PUBLISHERS
NEW YORK
NEW HAVEN   PHILADELPHIA

EDITOR-IN-CHIEF: Nancy Toff
EXECUTIVE EDITOR: Remmel T. Nunn
MANAGING EDITOR: Karyn Gullen Browne
COPY CHIEF: Juliann Barbato
PICTURE EDITOR: Adrian G. Allen
ART DIRECTOR: Giannella Garrett
MANUFACTURING MANAGER: Gerald Levine

Staff for JAMES I:

SENIOR EDITOR: John W. Selfridge
ASSISTANT EDITOR: Kathleen McDermott
COPY EDITOR: Karen Hammonds
EDITORIAL ASSISTANT: Sean Ginty
ASSOCIATE PICTURE EDITOR: Juliette Dickstein
PICTURE RESEARCHER: Amla Sangvi
SENIOR DESIGNER: Debby Jay
ASSISTANT DESIGNER: Jill Goldreyer
PRODUCTION COORDINATOR: Joseph Romano
COVER ILLUSTRATION: Richard Martin

CREATIVE DIRECTOR: Harold Steinberg

First Printing

1 3 5 7 9 8 6 4 2

Library of Congress Cataloging in Publication Data

Dwyer, Frank. JAMES I/Frank Dwyer.

p. cm.—(World leaders past & present)
Bibliography: p.
Includes index.
Summary: A biography of the son of Mary, Queen of Scots, who was the
first Stuart king of England, the sponsor of what is known as the King
James Version of the Bible, and the monarch responsible for the
migration of the Puritans to America in 1620.

ISBN 1-55546-811-X
1. James I, King of England, 1566–1625—Juvenile
literature. 2. Great Britain—History—James I, 1603–1625—
Juvenile literature. 3. Great Britain—Kings and rulers—
Biography—Juvenile literature. [1. James I, King of
England, 1566–1625. 2. Kings, queens, rulers, etc.] I. Title.
II. Series.
DA391.D88   1988   941.06′1′0924—dc 19 [B] [92] 87-
26579 CIP AC

Contents

John Adams
John Quincy Adams
Konrad Adenauer
Alexander the Great
Salvador Allende
Marc Antony
Corazon Aquino
Yasir Arafat
King Arthur
Hafez al-Assad
Kemal Atatürk
Attila
Clement Attlee
Augustus Caesar
Menachem Begin
David Ben-Gurion
Otto von Bismarck
Léon Blum
Simon Bolívar
Cesare Borgia
Willy Brandt
Leonid Brezhnev
Julius Caesar
John Calvin
Jimmy Carter
Fidel Castro
Catherine the Great
Charlemagne
Chiang Kai-Shek
Winston Churchill
Georges Clemenceau
Cleopatra
Constantine the Great
Hernán Cortés
Oliver Cromwell
Georges-Jacques
  Danton
Jefferson Davis
Moshe Dayan
Charles de Gaulle
Eamon De Valera
Eugene Debs
Deng Xiaoping
Benjamin Disraeli
Alexander Dubček
François & Jean-Claude
  Duvalier
Dwight Eisenhower
Eleanor of Aquitaine
Elizabeth i
Faisal
Ferdinand & Isabella
Francisco Franco
Benjamin Franklin

Frederick the Great
Indira Gandhi
Mohandas Gandhi
Giuseppe Garibaldi
Amin & Bashir Gemayel
Genghis Khan
William Gladstone
Mikhail Gorbachev
Ulysses S. Grant
Ernesto "Che" Guevara
Tenzin Gyatso
Alexander Hamilton
Dag Hammarskjöld
Henry viii
Henry of Navarre
Paul von Hindenburg
Hirohito
Adolf Hitler
Ho Chi Minh
King Hussein
Ivan the Terrible
Andrew Jackson
James i
Wojciech Jaruzelski
Thomas Jefferson
Joan of Arc
Pope John xxiii
Pope John Paul ii
Lyndon Johnson
Benito Juárez
John Kennedy
Robert Kennedy
Jomo Kenyatta
Ayatollah Khomeini
Nikita Khrushchev
Kim Il Sung
Martin Luther King, Jr.
Henry Kissinger
Kublai Khan
Lafayette
Robert E. Lee
Vladimir Lenin
Abraham Lincoln
David Lloyd George
Louis xiv
Martin Luther
Judas Maccabeus
James Madison
Nelson & Winnie
  Mandela
Mao Zedong
Ferdinand Marcos
George Marshall

Mary, Queen of Scots
Tomáš Masaryk
Golda Meir
Klemens von Metternich
James Monroe
Hosni Mubarak
Robert Mugabe
Benito Mussolini
Napoléon Bonaparte
Gamal Abdel Nasser
Jawaharlal Nehru
Nero
Nicholas II
Richard Nixon
Kwame Nkrumah
Daniel Ortega
Mohammed Reza Pahlavi
Thomas Paine
Charles Stewart
  Parnell
Pericles
Juan Perón
Peter the Great
Pol Pot
Muammar el-Qaddafi
Ronald Reagan
Cardinal Richelieu
Maximilien Robespierre
Eleanor Roosevelt
Franklin Roosevelt
Theodore Roosevelt
Anwar Sadat
Haile Selassie
Prince Sihanouk
Jan Smuts
Joseph Stalin
Sukarno
Sun Yat-sen
Tamerlane
Mother Teresa
Margaret Thatcher
Josip Broz Tito
Toussaint L'Ouverture
Leon Trotsky
Pierre Trudeau
Harry Truman
Queen Victoria
Lech Walesa
George Washington
Chaim Weizmann
Woodrow Wilson
Xerxes
Emiliano Zapata
Zhou Enlai

CHELSEA HOUSE PUBLISHERS

ON LEADERSHIP

Arthur M. Schlesinger, jr.

LEADERSHIP, it may be said, is really what makes the world go round. Love no doubt smooths the passage; but love is a private transaction between consenting adults. Leadership is a public transaction with history. The idea of leadership affirms the capacity of individuals to move, inspire, and mobilize masses of people so that they act together in pursuit of an end. Sometimes leadership serves good purposes, sometimes bad; but whether the end is benign or evil, great leaders are those men and women who leave their personal stamp on history.

Now, the very concept of leadership implies the proposition that individuals can make a difference. This proposition has never been universally accepted. From classical times to the present day, eminent thinkers have regarded individuals as no more than the agents and pawns of larger forces, whether the gods and goddesses of the ancient world or, in the modern era, race, class, nation, the dialectic, the will of the people, the spirit of the times, history itself. Against such forces, the individual dwindles into insignificance.

So contends the thesis of historical determinism. Tolstoy's great novel *War and Peace* offers a famous statement of the case. Why, Tolstoy asked, did millions of men in the Napoleonic Wars, denying their human feelings and their common sense, move back and forth across Europe slaughtering their fellows? "The war," Tolstoy answered, "was bound to happen simply because it was bound to happen." All prior history predetermined it. As for leaders, they, Tolstoy said, "are but the labels that serve to give a name to an end and, like labels, they have the least possible connection with the event." The greater the leader, "the more conspicuous the inevitability and the predestination of every act he commits." The leader, said Tolstoy, is "the slave of history."

Determinism takes many forms. Marxism is the determinism of class. Nazism the determinism of race. But the idea of men and women as the slaves of history runs athwart the deepest human instincts. Rigid determinism abolishes the idea of human freedom—

the assumption of free choice that underlies every move we make, every word we speak, every thought we think. It abolishes the idea of human responsibility, since it is manifestly unfair to reward or punish people for actions that are by definition beyond their control. No one can live consistently by any deterministic creed. The Marxist states prove this themselves by their extreme susceptibility to the cult of leadership.

More than that, history refutes the idea that individuals make no difference. In December 1931 a British politician crossing Park Avenue in New York City between 76th and 77th Streets around 10:30 P.M. looked in the wrong direction and was knocked down by an automobile—a moment, he later recalled, of a man aghast, a world aglare: "I do not understand why I was not broken like an eggshell or squashed like a gooseberry." Fourteen months later an American politician, sitting in an open car in Miami, Florida, was fired on by an assassin; the man beside him was hit. Those who believe that individuals make no difference to history might well ponder whether the next two decades would have been the same had Mario Constasino's car killed Winston Churchill in 1931 and Giuseppe Zangara's bullet killed Franklin Roosevelt in 1933. Suppose, in addition, that Adolf Hitler had been killed in the street fighting during the Munich *Putsch* of 1923 and that Lenin had died of typhus during World War I. What would the 20th century be like now?

For better or for worse, individuals do make a difference. "The notion that a people can run itself and its affairs anonymously," wrote the philosopher William James, "is now well known to be the silliest of absurdities. Mankind does nothing save through initiatives on the part of inventors, great or small, and imitation by the rest of us—these are the sole factors in human progress. Individuals of genius show the way, and set the patterns, which common people then adopt and follow."

Leadership, James suggests, means leadership in thought as well as in action. In the long run, leaders in thought may well make the greater difference to the world. But, as Woodrow Wilson once said, "Those only are leaders of men, in the general eye, who lead in action. . . . It is at their hands that new thought gets its translation into the crude language of deeds." Leaders in thought often invent in solitude and obscurity, leaving to later generations the tasks of imitation. Leaders in action—the leaders portrayed in this series—have to be effective in their own time.

And they cannot be effective by themselves. They must act in response to the rhythms of their age. Their genius must be adapted, in a phrase of William James's, "to the receptivities of the moment." Leaders are useless without followers. "There goes the mob," said the French politician hearing a clamor in the streets. "I am their leader. I must follow them." Great leaders turn the inchoate emotions of the mob to purposes of their own. They seize on the opportunities of their time, the hopes, fears, frustrations, crises, potentialities. They succeed when events have prepared the way for them, when the community is awaiting to be aroused, when they can provide the clarifying and organizing ideas. Leadership ignites the circuit between the individual and the mass and thereby alters history.

It may alter history for better or for worse. Leaders have been responsible for the most extravagant follies and most monstrous crimes that have beset suffering humanity. They have also been vital in such gains as humanity has made in individual freedom, religious and racial tolerance, social justice, and respect for human rights.

There is no sure way to tell in advance who is going to lead for good and who for evil. But a glance at the gallery of men and women in *World Leaders—Past and Present* suggests some useful tests.

One test is this: Do leaders lead by force or by persuasion? By command or by consent? Through most of history leadership was exercised by the divine right of authority. The duty of followers was to defer and to obey. "Theirs not to reason why / Theirs but to do and die." On occasion, as with the so-called enlightened despots of the 18th century in Europe, absolutist leadership was animated by humane purposes. More often, absolutism nourished the passion for domination, land, gold, and conquest and resulted in tyranny.

The great revolution of modern times has been the revolution of equality. The idea that all people should be equal in their legal condition has undermined the old structure of authority, hierarchy, and deference. The revolution of equality has had two contrary effects on the nature of leadership. For equality, as Alexis de Tocqueville pointed out in his great study *Democracy in America*, might mean equality in servitude as well as equality in freedom.

"I know of only two methods of establishing equality in the political world," Tocqueville wrote. "Rights must be given to every citizen, or none at all to anyone . . . save one, who is the master of all." There was no middle ground "between the sovereignty of all and the absolute power of one man." In his astonishing prediction of 20th-century totalitarian dictatorship, Tocqueville explained how the revolution of equality could lead to the *"Führerprinzip"* and more terrible absolutism than the world had ever known.

But when rights are given to every citizen and the sovereignty of all is established, the problem of leadership takes a new form, becomes more exacting than ever before. It is easy to issue commands and enforce them by the rope and the stake, the concentration camp and the *gulag.* It is much harder to use argument and achievement to overcome opposition and win consent. The Founding Fathers of the United States understood the difficulty. They believed that history had given them the opportunity to decide, as Alexander Hamilton wrote in the first Federalist Paper, whether men are indeed capable of basing government on "reflection and choice, or whether they are forever destined to depend . . . on accident and force."

Government by reflection and choice called for a new style of leadership and a new quality of followership. It required leaders to be responsive to popular concerns, and it required followers to be active and informed participants in the process. Democracy does not eliminate emotion from politics; sometimes it fosters demagoguery; but it is confident that, as the greatest of democratic leaders put it, you cannot fool all of the people all of the time. It measures leadership by results and retires those who overreach or falter or fail.

It is true that in the long run despots are measured by results too. But they can postpone the day of judgment, sometimes indefinitely, and in the meantime they can do infinite harm. It is also true that democracy is no guarantee of virtue and intelligence in government, for the voice of the people is not necessarily the voice of God. But democracy, by assuring the right of opposition, offers built-in resistance to the evils inherent in absolutism. As the theologian Reinhold Niebuhr summed it up, "Man's capacity for justice makes democracy possible, but man's inclination to injustice makes democracy necessary."

A second test for leadership is the end for which power is sought. When leaders have as their goal the supremacy of a master race or the promotion of totalitarian revolution or the acquisition and exploitation of colonies or the protection of greed and privilege or the preservation of personal power, it is likely that their leadership will do little to advance the cause of humanity. When their goal is the abolition of slavery, the liberation of women, the enlargement of opportunity for the poor and powerless, the extension of equal rights to racial minorities, the defense of the freedoms of expression and opposition, it is likely that their leadership will increase the sum of human liberty and welfare.

Leaders have done great harm to the world. They have also conferred great benefits. You will find both sorts in this series. Even "good" leaders must be regarded with a certain wariness. Leaders are not demigods; they put on their trousers one leg after another just like ordinary mortals. No leader is infallible, and every leader needs to be reminded of this at regular intervals. Irreverence irritates leaders but is their salvation. Unquestioning submission corrupts leaders and demeans followers. Making a cult of a leader is always a mistake. Fortunately hero worship generates its own antidote. "Every hero," said Emerson, "becomes a bore at last."

The signal benefit the great leaders confer is to embolden the rest of us to live according to our own best selves, to be active, insistent, and resolute in affirming our own sense of things. For great leaders attest to the reality of human freedom against the supposed inevitabilities of history. And they attest to the wisdom and power that may lie within the most unlikely of us, which is why Abraham Lincoln remains the supreme example of great leadership. A great leader, said Emerson, exhibits new possibilities to all humanity. "We feed on genius. . . . Great men exist that there may be greater men."

Great leaders, in short, justify themselves by emancipating and empowering their followers. So humanity struggles to master its destiny, remembering with Alexis de Tocqueville: "It is true that around every man a fatal circle is traced beyond which he cannot pass; but within the wide verge of that circle he is powerful and free; as it is with man, so with communities."

1

The Pretty Queen

Scotland is a divided land. A range of great hills cuts across the middle of the country on a sharp diagonal. North of that line are the harsh, remote Highlands, once an exotic world of independent chieftains, passionate clan loyalties, and endless private feuds and wars. Here the chivalric spirit and the feudal practices of the Middle Ages continued to thrive long after most countries in Europe had moved on to the centralization of power in a monarch and the sharing of that power with a representative assembly. South of the Highland line, the rich soil of the Lowlands helped create prosperity and progress. Along the troubled border between Scotland and its powerful, dangerous southern neighbor, England, a sort of Highland anarchy prevailed. Scotland, to protect itself from mighty England, sought alliance with England's traditional enemy, France, which meant for England the constant threat of invasion from the north. Savage raids back and forth across the border were commonplace for centuries. The productive Lowlands, which included the great capital of Edinburgh on the Firth of Forth, came to represent the hope of the future for Scotland.

The royal family of Scotland, the Stewarts, took its name from an ancestral title: High Stewarts (or Stewards) of Scotland stood next in power to the

> *Her chances of ruling that wild and lawless kingdom with any success had been small at best, and her character and conduct reduced such chances to zero.*
> —D. HARRIS WILLSON
> historian, on Mary's reign
> in Scotland

Mary, Queen of Scots, holds her infant son, James. Born in 1566 amidst rumors of illegitimacy and under the cloud of Mary's deepening feud with the Protestant lords of Scotland, James was forever separated from his mother when she was captured and imprisoned in 1567.

Scotland in the 16th century was a harsh land. Its wind-swept hills and boggy moors were the sites of battles between rival nobles in what was still a largely feudal society.

early kings. The Stewarts fought long and hard to establish the authority of their crown, but the peculiar combination of independent Highlanders and interfering Englishmen continually defeated them. In divided Scotland, anarchy prevailed, and Stewart kings often died young.

On November 23, 1542, English forces defeated King James V of Scotland at the Battle of Solway Moss. About two weeks later the brokenhearted king had to bear another disappointment when his queen, Mary of Guise, gave birth to a daughter. The double shock was too much for him; James died a week later. His infant daughter, Mary, became queen of Scotland. King Henry VIII of England tried to arrange a marriage for little Mary Stewart and his young son, Edward, but the Scots felt that such a union would only subjugate them to their enemy. Instead, they turned again to the "auld alliance" with France, betrothed Mary to the dauphin, the son of the French king, and sent her to France to be educated. In Scotland the forces led by the independent and vocal Protestant Reform church opposed the pro-French regency of the Catholic queen mother and leaned toward England.

Henry VIII's only surviving child, Elizabeth, ascended the throne of England in 1558. Catholic Europe had never accepted Henry's divorce of his first wife to marry Elizabeth's mother, Anne Boleyn, and his subsequent divorce from Anne had "illegitimized" Elizabeth. As a result, Catholic Europe — France, Spain, the Papal States — did not recognize Elizabeth as the true queen of England. She held her power at the will and pleasure of her own Protestant countrymen, but to many, the 15-year-old queen of Scotland had a stronger claim to the English crown. Mary Stuart (the spelling of the family name had changed while the young queen lived in France) was the granddaughter of Henry VIII's sister Margaret.

In 1558, when Mary was 16, she and the sickly dauphin were married, and a year later he inherited his father's crown as King Francis II. Mary had been queen of France for a year and a half when her husband died. The 18-year-old widow — tall, slender, beautiful, elegant, and devoutly Catholic — returned to a divided land that she had left as a child, and to a difficult, quarrelsome, dangerous people she would never really know or understand. She spoke French, and her manners and ideas reflected the ease and grace of the French court. In her absence, Calvinism, a particularly austere religion preached by John Calvin in Geneva, had made a deep impression on the Scots. The great leader of the Calvinist congregation, or Kirk, in Scotland was the eloquent, fiercely independent John Knox. Many of the most powerful lords of Scotland embraced Calvinism.

Knox and his followers were bitterly hostile to the Catholic queen. Her domestic difficulties were compounded by her relationship with Queen Elizabeth, who constantly meddled in the affairs of Scotland. Nevertheless, Mary's rule began well. Her brother James, earl of Moray, served her ably, as did the shrewd statesman William Maitland of Lethington. Her sorrows began four years later, when she married her 19-year-old English cousin, Henry Stewart, Lord Darnley. Darnley, a Catholic, was also descended from Margaret Tudor and had his own

Raised in the royal court of France by her mother's family of Guise, Mary Stuart learned manners and customs alien to her native Scotland. When she married Francis, the heir to the French throne, in 1558, Mary expected to remain at the lively, sophisticated court she loved.

Calvinist minister John Knox preaches to Queen Mary. The fiery leader of the Scottish Protestant congregation — known as the Kirk — Knox bitterly opposed Mary's desire to restore Catholicism to Scotland.

claim to the English crown. Despite the furious opposition of Elizabeth and the strong displeasure of the Scottish Kirk and the Protestant lords, Mary married Darnley on July 29, 1565.

The Protestants, led by Moray, took to the field. Mary had the support of powerful Highland Catholics, and she called James Hepburn, earl of Bothwell, to serve as commander of her troops. Mary and her soldiers rode around the countryside seeking the elusive Moray, and sometime during the course of these "Chase About Raids," she conceived her only child.

When Moray escaped across the border to England, Mary began to dream of overthrowing the obstreperous Kirk and restoring Catholicism in Scotland. Many who did not rise up to fight beside Moray began to regret the ascendancy of the pro-Vatican forces, and the Protestant lords grew increasingly disaffected. On March 9, 1566, while Mary was having dinner with a few close companions in her private dining room at Holyrood Palace, a gang of armed men suddenly broke in. They had come for Mary's close friend and companion, an Italian court musician named David Rizzio. The queen, six months pregnant, was held to one side as the intruders brutally murdered Rizzio. Mary feared for her own life and her child's. She was spared but held prisoner in her own castle.

Mary cleverly convinced Darnley, who had played a part in the conspiracy, to help her escape. Despite her advanced pregnancy, Mary rode, with Darnley, 30 miles to Bothwell's castle. The Catholic lords rallied to her side, and the Protestant conspirators fled the country. Mary now worked to restore her own government. Though she had come to loathe the king, she understood the necessity of keeping him beside her.

On the morning of June 19, 1566, after a difficult labor, Mary gave birth to a son, James. When King Henry came to see the baby, Mary publicly denied the widespread rumor that James was Rizzio's. Mary also voiced the hope that her son would be the first to unite the kingdoms of Scotland and England.

Prince James was christened in the chapel at Stirling Castle on December 15, 1566. His absent godparents — both of whom sent splendid gifts — were the king of France and the queen of England. Mary had given her Protestant lords rich new taffeta suits for the christening, but their religion did not permit them to enter the chapel, so they watched from the doorway as the Catholic lords accompanied the baby to the font. A week after the prince's baptism, Mary signed a proclamation allowing the return of Moray and his supporters.

In late January 1567 Mary had her husband, who was ill, brought to the outskirts of Edinburgh and installed in a small but substantial house at a place called Kirk o' Field. In the early hours of February 10, a huge explosion rocked the city. The king and his page were found dead in the garden. They had not been killed in the blast but apparently were smothered earlier.

The queen's favorite, Bothwell, although himself the chief suspect, took aggressive charge of the investigation. Mary did not pretend to a grief she did

In 1565 Mary wed her cousin Henry Stuart, Lord Darnley. The marriage roused the ire of two enemies Mary could ill afford to antagonize: The Kirk opposed Darnley because he was English and Catholic; Queen Elizabeth of England feared that the union strengthened Mary's claim to the English throne.

not feel, but she shocked those around her when she entertained herself with a round of golf. Moray, disturbed by the new tone of the court, announced his retirement and went abroad. At Bothwell's trial for the king's murder, his men roamed the streets of Edinburgh, no accusers came forward to confront him, and he was acquitted.

In March, Mary took James to Stirling Castle and left him in the care of the earl and countess of Mar; the earls of Mar were the traditional guardians of Stuart royalty. On April 22 the queen came to Stirling with a small entourage to visit her son. It would be the last time she would ever see him. James was just 10 months old; he would not remember his remarkable mother. On April 24, as she returned to Edinburgh, she was intercepted by a large band of armed men led by Bothwell, who abducted her and forced her to marry him.

The union with the widely despised Bothwell was the final undoing of Mary. Many people believed she had conspired with him to murder the king and then fake her own abduction in order to marry him. On June 15 a large force of Protestant rebels met Bothwell's army at Carberry Hill. Deserted by his men, Bothwell agreed to surrender Mary to the Prot-

After the sudden death of her husband, King Francis II, Mary returned to Scotland in 1561 to claim her throne. Although the Scottish Protestant nobles duly greeted their new queen, many were apprehensive about her staunch Catholicism.

estant leaders. She kissed Bothwell good-bye before the armies (she would never see him again) and was spirited away to a lonely tower on an island in Loch Leven.

A new wave of Protestant activism followed. John Knox reappeared to thunder in his pulpit: He demanded Mary's death. The discovery of a silver casket full of what seemed to be Mary's love letters to Bothwell finished the blackening of her character, because they clearly implicated her in King Henry's murder. (On textual grounds, copies of these Casket Letters have been dismissed as forgeries; the originals disappeared mysteriously in 1600.) Queen Elizabeth, who did not like the idea of subjects determining their monarch's fate, threatened an invasion if Mary was harmed, and she directed that Prince James be sent to England, where she could bring him up in safety. The Scottish lords refused to release the prince.

On July 25 the rebel lords threatened Mary with a trial and reminded her that a woman's punishment for the crime of adultery was public burning. They persuaded the queen to surrender her crown. The earl of Mar brought Prince James down from Stirling Castle to the village church, where the triumphant rebels had him proclaimed king on July 29, 1567. James's uncle, Moray, returned to Scotland to govern as regent for the young king.

King James VI of Scotland, conceived on a battlefield, threatened in the womb by an assassin's pistol, crowned by men who had murdered his father, and preached over by the minister who clamored for his mother's death, was only 13 months old, too young to understand any of these turbulent events. During his life, he would not be able to remember a time before he was king.

Defeated and captured by the Protestant lords in 1567 and threatened with trial and execution, Mary is forced to sign her abdication. On July 29, 1567, her son, under a Protestant regency, became King James VI of Scotland.

2

The Weeping Boy

In the first year of the reign of the infant king, the Scottish parliament, under the influence of Moray and the Protestant lords, reaffirmed the acts of the so-called Reformation Parliament of 1560, which established Protestantism as the official religion of the land. The regent worked to establish order and win general support for his rule. In March 1568 the new stability was gravely threatened when Mary escaped from Loch Leven. The Highland clans, the disaffected Catholics, and the enemies of Moray and his circle all rallied to her. She could also hope for support from Spain, France, even from England: The defense of any ruler against forced abdication was every monarch's cause. However, the foreign support never materialized, and in May 1568 the Protestant forces routed Mary's troops at Langside. The desperate queen fled across Solway Firth to throw herself on the uncertain mercy of Elizabeth.

Elizabeth insisted that Mary clear herself of the grave charges of conspiracy to murder her husband. At a commission set up by Elizabeth nothing was proved against Mary, but the Casket Letters and the constant rumors blackened her reputation. The earls of Northumberland and Westmorland raised a rebellion in the north of England with the intention of liberating Mary and restoring the old Catholic

I was alone, without father or mother, brother or sister, king of the realm, and heir apparent of England.
—KING JAMES I
reflecting on his childhood

The young King James of Scotland had a difficult, lonely childhood under the stern care of his mother's Protestant enemies. He reportedly slept "in a gloomy bed of black damask, the ruff, headpieces, and pillows being fringed with black."

In May 1568 Mary, disguised as a servant, escaped from her island prison and gathered an army. Her troops, however, were defeated at Langside in Scotland, and desperate to avoid imprisonment again, Mary fled to England to seek asylum with Queen Elizabeth.

faith. Elizabeth put down the rebellion with great severity and decided to hold on to Mary, who would be a prisoner for the remaining 19 years of her life.

The departure of the pretty queen was hardly enough to transform volatile Scotland into a calm and peaceful land. The growing power of Moray and the Kirk soon awoke opposition. Maitland of Lethington, Kirkcaldy of Grange, and various Catholic lords took up Mary's cause. In Linlithgow, on the morning of January 11, 1570, Moray was shot and killed by a hidden assassin. His murder signaled the outbreak of a civil war.

The queen's party, led by Lethington, held Edinburgh. The Protestant lords held some major castles and, more importantly, the young king himself. They named James's grandfather, Matthew Stewart, earl of Lennox, to the regency. On September 3, 1571, when a party of queen's men led by Kirkcaldy of Grange attacked the Protestant camp, Lennox was mortally wounded. The bleeding regent was carried into the castle past his frightened five-year-old grandson. "All is well if the babe is well," Lennox said. He died the following day. James never forgot that bloody night; he would have a great fear and horror of sudden violence all his life. His guardian, the earl of Mar, succeeded Lennox as regent.

Mar lasted little more than a year before he died on November 24, 1572. John Knox, worn out by his hard life and his tireless, thundering fanaticism, died the same day. James Douglas, earl of Morton, perhaps the most selfish and treacherous — certainly the strongest — of all the Protestant lords, took over as regent and quickly ended the war. After Morton conquered Edinburgh Castle in April 1573, Lethington killed himself, and Kirkcaldy of Grange was hanged. The power of the queen seemed finally broken.

Morton's blunt, fearless, autocratic style provided the country with its first extended period of calm in a long time. Morton served from 1572 to 1578, maintaining law and order in a land where anarchy and violence had prevailed. James grew up in these relatively tranquil years, and he doubtless learned about ruling a country from the pragmatic, authoritarian regent.

The king was a most diligent scholar at all his

James Stuart, earl of Moray and stepbrother to Mary, was the first of four regents to rule Scotland during James's childhood. When he was assassinated in January 1570, a struggle erupted again between Mary's supporters and the Protestant lords.

George Buchanan, a well-known Renaissance man of letters, served as James's principal tutor. Under Buchanan's rigorous instruction, James became a diligent scholar, and visitors were surprised at the advanced learning mastered by such a young boy.

lessons, and his lonely, difficult childhood was dominated by the imposing figure of his tutor, George Buchanan. Buchanan had studied and lectured in Paris. The cultivated and witty Renaissance scholar had been a good friend to Mary on her return to Scotland, but then he had turned Protestant with all the passion of a learned convert. He became bitterly hostile to the queen and wrote a scathing denunciation of her.

James was four years old when Buchanan took charge of his education. The elderly scholar was a rude, mean-hearted, bad-tempered schoolmaster, but his energy and drive turned James into a scholar, too. The young king studied Greek before breakfast (after his morning prayers, of course), Latin or history before lunch, and arithmetic, geography, astronomy, and rhetoric (writing and speaking) in the afternoon. Buchanan's assistant, a young theology scholar from Geneva named Peter Young, instructed James in Calvinist doctrine. More importantly, he befriended the lonely little boy. James had nightmares all his life about Buchanan, but he was always grateful for the rare kindness shown him by Young.

The royal tutors produced a boy of prodigious learning. An ambassador from Elizabeth left a vivid picture of James at the age of eight: "He speaketh the French tongue marvelous well; and that which seems strange to me, he was able *ex tempore* [without preparation] . . . to read a chapter of the Bible out of Latin into French, and out of French after into English, so well, as few men could have added anything to his translation. . . . They also made his Highness dance before me, which he likewise did with a very good grace; a Prince sure of great hope, if God give him life."

The mention of his dancing is something of a surprise, because James had one foot turned in, perhaps as the result of a case of rickets (a disease that softens and deforms growing bones) that was neglected in the violent confusion of his early childhood. All his life he moved in a clumsy, circular gait. He loved to ride, however, and hunting became a keen and lifelong pleasure.

James's childhood must have been a stifling, love-less one. In her first year out of Scotland, Mary sent the boy a pony, but because she addressed her letter to "my dear son, James Charles, Prince of Scotland" instead of "King James," he was not allowed to keep the gift. Two years later the Scottish parliament forbade all communication between mother and son. Buchanan's frequent ugly remarks about Mary and his severe discipline, including punishment with the rod, did not make life any easier for the political orphan. In such harsh surroundings it is little wonder that James grew up with his spirit somewhat maimed.

Though learned in matters of scholarship, James was never schooled in the manners and graces suited to his royal state. A later observer would write that "in speaking and eating, in his dress and in his sports, in his conversation in the presence of women, his manners are crude and uncivil and display a lack of proper instruction." The sour old bachelor Buchanan cared nothing for such things.

Whatever the perils of Buchanan's regimen, James — and Scotland — had six years of relative peace under Morton. The regent's very success, however, was enough to unite his enemies. In March 1578 two powerful Highland chieftains, the Catholic earls of Atholl and Argyll, appeared before the adolescent king. Outmaneuvering Morton, who tried to convince the king that the Highland earls were worthless rebels, Atholl and Argyll persuaded James to begin ruling Scotland in his own right. On March 12, 1578, Scotland's King James VI "accepted the Government."

The ascendancy of the Catholic earls was short-lived. John Erskine, the new earl of Mar and a childhood friend of James's, entered Stirling Castle with a band of armed men to assert his claim to be guardian. In the ensuing "ruffle," as the Scots called it, blood was shed and Mar gained control of the frightened king. Morton summoned a parliament to ratify this easy coup, and James was required to assure the parliament that he freely accepted the return of Morton. Morton's enemies were ready to contest it, but James had no stomach for fighting.

> *Awkward in his person and ungainly in his manners, he was ill qualified to command respect; partial and undiscerning in his affections, he was little fitted to acquire general love.*
> —DAVID HUME
> historian, on James

These events attracted the attention of Catholic Europe, which believed that James was still sympathetic to his mother and her party. The Catholic duke of Guise, the de facto ruler of France under King Henry III, thought the time might be ripe to renew the "auld alliance." Perhaps the impressionable young king of Scotland could be won back to the Catholic faith. Perhaps, eventually, he might bring England with him.

Guise sent an emissary to the court in Edinburgh. Esmé Stuart, seigneur d'Aubigny, was a youthful 37-year-old distant cousin of James's. Tall and handsome, with a red beard, pale face, and flashing eyes, he brought something of the wit, ease, and polish of Paris to the grim northern court of the backward and ill-bred prodigy. He was unfailingly gentle, charming, and tender to the young king, and the lonely, love-starved boy soon adored him.

James celebrated his 13th birthday, and on Oc-

James and the Scottish royal court made their headquarters at Edinburgh. The walled capital city was set in a rough valley punctuated by craggy hills.

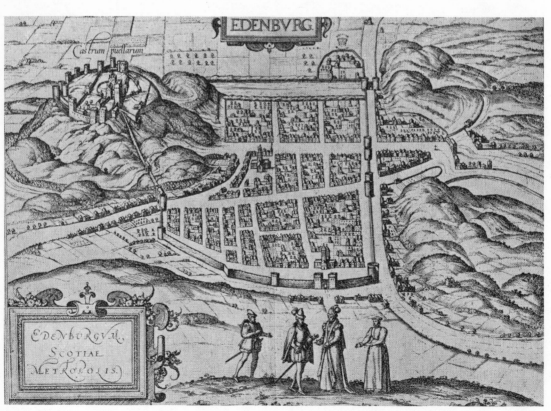

tober 17, 1579, he made a grand triumphal entry, welcomed with jolly pageants and orations, into Edinburgh. D'Aubigny rode beside him. The Frenchman's power and influence grew rapidly as James made him earl, then duke of Lennox, and the remnants of the queen's party, with all of Morton's enemies, gathered around him. James was happier than he had ever been.

Morton, bitter and contemptuous, was rarely seen at court. Long in league with England, he waited in vain for help from Elizabeth. On December 31, 1580, the Lennox faction struck at Morton when Captain James Stewart, a bold, masterful soldier of fortune who commanded the king's new bodyguard, accused Morton of complicity in the murder of James's father, nearly 14 years earlier. Morton was arrested, and no one lifted a hand to save him. He spent six months in irons and in June 1581 was executed on a treason conviction. When Elizabeth heard the news, she was furious with young King James: "That false Scotch urchin! What can be expected from the double dealing of such an urchin as this?"

James and his companions rejoiced in their new freedom. The king made Captain Stewart earl of Arran, and he let Lennox and Arran run the government while he hunted and wrote poetry and tried to make up for all the years of deprivation with new amusements. Lennox apparently became his lover: James embraced him in public, and a contemporary chronicler reported on the relationship in the careful language of the day: "His Majesty having conceived an inward affection to the Lord d'Aubigny, entered in great familiarity and quiet purposes with him." The two spent their time in exquisite theological discussions, and Lennox, seemingly convinced by James's arguments, publicly converted to Protestantism. They also indulged in the bawdy joking and blaspheming for which their circle was becoming notorious. George Buchanan had taught James that a king derived his power from his people, and that the people have a right to topple a tyrant. Lennox now taught his eager pupil a different lesson: A king's power was derived from God

French emissary Esmé Stuart, a distant cousin to James, was sent to Edinburgh to strengthen Franco-Scottish ties. The handsome courtier, who befriended the lonely adolescent king, rose quickly in James's favor and was appointed duke of Lennox in 1580.

and was not to be challenged by his subjects. This grand French vision of absolute monarchy was most appealing to the adolescent king.

While James dallied, Lennox dreamed great dreams and hatched great plots. He concocted a fantastic scheme to invade England and free Mary so mother and son could rule together in Scotland. The Kirk, shocked by the king's behavior and afraid of Lennox's influence, spoke out with renewed vigor. The Protestant lords, men who had been lying low since the fall of Morton, began to stir.

In late August 1582 James went hunting in the neighborhood of Ruthven Castle, the home of William Ruthven, the earl of Gowrie. The earl was a leader of the disaffected Protestants — the Lords of the Enterprise, as they called themselves. Gowrie invited the king to spend the night at Ruthven, and the innocent James agreed. When he tried to depart the next morning, he found the master of Glamis, Thomas Lyon, barring his way: The Lords of the Enterprise had kidnapped him. Angry and frightened, James began to weep. The master of Glamis said coldly, "Better that boys should weep than bearded men."

The king's foolish behavior had left him sadly isolated. Lennox had no real power to attempt his rescue; Arran, magnificent and absurd, rode off alone

The Gowrie House was home to William Ruthven, earl of Gowrie, who led the Lords of the Enterprise, a group of nobles opposed to the growing influence on James of the duke of Lennox. In 1582 the Lords kidnapped James, who was forced to send Lennox back to France.

An idealized portrait of Mary, Queen of Scots, shows her as a tender, loving mother to James. In reality, James was a confirmed Protestant who did not wish to see his mother return to claim the throne he now occupied.

to save the king and was easily taken. Balked of his fantasies, Lennox lingered in Edinburgh until December, but the Kirk condemned him, the people cursed him, and his continued presence endangered the king. Finally, with great sorrow, James urged Lennox to go back to France. The king of Scotland never saw his beloved friend again; Lennox died shortly after his return.

3

A Dangerous World

James, who had been so happy, plunged into despair. He felt humiliated, betrayed, angry, and afraid. The Lords of the Enterprise meant him no physical harm — they needed him to legitimize their coup — but their authority was hateful to him. They forced him to proclaim the treachery of Lennox and then to declare a free and independent Kirk. They guarded him strictly. Though James shouted and wept, Gowrie would not even let him go riding. When a Protestant preacher denounced him publicly, James wept. Helpless and furious, the captive king called the Protestant ministers "a pack of knaves," vowing that "he had rather lose his kingdom than not be avenged on them." He developed a lifelong loathing for the brazen Kirkmen.

This period of imprisonment, however unpleasant, did the young king some good by completing his political education. At Ruthven Castle he came to understand the harsh reality that without money and strong institutions to support his rule, a king's authority depended entirely on the loyalties he could command. His own situation in Scotland, though personally precarious, was strengthened by the relatively equal power of all the conflicting forces around him. The triumph of one party, or one man, inevitably created a substantial opposition. So

The psychological effect on James of this cruel blighting of his youthful affections may be imagined. Perhaps first love is rarely destined to end happily, but few experiences can have ended as desolately as that of James Stuart.
—ANTONIA FRASER
English author, on the forced dismissal of James's favorite, the duke of Lennox

Mary, left, rebuffs Queen Elizabeth as a servant tries to restrain her. Although Elizabeth treated her with leniency, Mary made herself a martyr to the Catholic cause and refused to renounce her claim to the English throne.

James learned to wait, to dissemble, to play all factions and parties against each other, and to trust no one. As his boyhood ended, he began to work diligently to achieve two goals: to gain his freedom from all factions and rule Scotland with independent authority; and to secure for himself the precious inheritance of the English crown.

Patience helped solve his immediate problem. The Lords of the Enterprise found it increasingly expensive to hold him. James seemed resigned to his captivity, and their vigilance slackened. In June 1583, not 10 months after Lennox had made the same mistake, the Ruthven lords let James go hunting without adequate guard. While hunting, the king received an invitation from his uncle the earl of March, and James rode hard for the castle at St. Andrews, where the Lennox faction awaited him.

James was once more in the hands of the Catholics. Most of the Ruthven lords fled the country. Gowrie himself knelt to the king and begged forgiveness. James forgave him, because he was now shrewd enough to realize that an absolute triumph by either party would diminish his own authority. He was less gracious to a delegation from the Kirk. No other king would have borne so much from them, he said, but the Kirkmen were unrepentant.

With all the heady excitement of a sheltered adolescent suddenly set free, James surrounded himself with congenial spirits and turned to his old pleasures: hunting, drinking, and writing poems. In 1584 he published his first book, the plodding and unoriginal *Essayes of a Prentise in the Divine Art of Poesie*. His own awkward metronomical efforts, *His Majesties Poeticall Exercises at Vacant Houres*, were written at this period but not published until 1591.

James left the daily business of government to the superb, arrogant, charismatic earl of Arran. Arran's high-handedness alienated everyone, and once again the Scottish court seethed with factions. Queen Elizabeth sent her talented treasurer, Francis Walsingham, to offer James a regular allowance if he would discard Arran and restore the Protestant

lords. James bristled: He hoped Elizabeth would allow him to choose his own councilors, as he allowed her to choose hers. Walsingham responded sharply, commenting on James's youth, lack of power, and good fortune in having such a friend as Elizabeth. He warned him pointedly of the danger of losing his throne.

James appealed for aid to all the Catholic powers: to King Henry III of France, King Philip II of Spain, the powerful duke of Guise, and to the pope. Frightened by Walsingham's ire and the broiling discontent at his own court, James sought the precarious security of some great Catholic power that could use Scotland as a base to attack Elizabeth.

In April 1584 the domestic crisis erupted. Some of the Ruthven lords had come back, and they now attempted another coup. After capturing Stirling Castle, however, they found themselves isolated: The people of Scotland did not flock to their standard, and the queen of England sent them no aid. Arran, a resolute warrior, soon routed them. Some fled over the border to England; others, including poor Gowrie, who had played no part in this rising, were hanged. Gowrie's estates were awarded to Arran.

James had triumphed over his political opponents, and now he achieved a comparable success against his religious enemies, thanks to the efforts of an extraordinary councilor, James Maitland of Thirlestane. Maitland saw his opportunity when the fiery leader of the Kirk, Andrew Melville, went too

The Tower of London, on the Thames River, was only one of Mary's prison homes for the 19 years she was in England. In 1586 the former queen of Scotland was convicted of conspiracy to murder Queen Elizabeth and place herself on the throne.

far in his preaching. Melville asserted that in spiritual matters, the king was no greater than any other man. The Bible, he said, was the minister's ultimate authority, higher even than the king's council. Melville somehow managed to escape arrest and fled to England. While the Kirk was leaderless, Maitland persuaded James to call a parliament, which met in May 1584. This anti-Kirk assembly proceeded to pass the so-called black acts, which proclaimed the king head of the Scottish church, with complete authority over all ecclesiastical matters. The Kirk could hold no general assembly without the king's permission, and preachers were forbidden to meddle in state matters. The king would appoint bishops — a papist practice abhorred by the Kirkmen. Furthermore, the Kirk would have to support a new royal bodyguard. A tax would be levied on all church benefices (income-producing offices or properties), and all vacant benefices would revert to the crown. Many Kirkmen fled to England, where they published pamphlets declaring that James was the illegitimate son of David Rizzio and not a real king at all, a slander that always made him weep with rage.

With the Protestant lords and the Kirkmen under control, all James needed at this point was someone to resolve his foreign policy crisis. Such a man appeared in the proud and allegedly beauteous person of Patrick, master of Gray. A former adviser of Mary's, Gray switched his loyalty to James and persuaded him to patch things up with Elizabeth. He pointed out that James did not have the strength or resources to oppose her successfully and suggested that he might achieve by alliance what he could never gain by conquest.

Gray rose quickly in James's esteem and affection. He was made a gentleman of the bedchamber — one of the privileged positions at the court because of the ready access to the king — and soon he was sharing the monarch's bed. When Elizabeth began discussions of a possible treaty, James sent Gray to London to represent him. At about the same time, Mary sent her own man to Scotland to learn

> *[James VI] was effective precisely because he had not attempted new and autocratic policies toward nobility, because he had not tried to undermine their political position.*
>
> —JENNIFER M. BROWN
> Scottish historian,
> on James's success
> in Scotland

about the character and plans of her son. He reported that James had three major defects: He was overconfident, he displayed an "indiscreet and wilful love for his favorites," and he was self-indulgent and lazy. Mary was horrified to learn of Gray's negotiations to bring about an Anglo-Scottish alliance that would leave her in captivity, and she poured out her complaints in a letter to James. He replied disdainfully that he had never agreed to a joint rule with her. He never wrote her again.

Elizabeth sent an ambassador to Scotland in May 1585 to offer James a treaty with a pension of 4,000 pounds a year. Maitland pressed diligently to get better terms for James, but Gray prevailed. James was thrilled with the treaty, which gave him a security, an authority, and an income he had never had before. Gray's triumph, however, was brief. This elegant champion of the English alliance was about to be sacrificed in the collision of greater destinies.

Since her confinement in England, Mary had been a focus for disaffected English Catholics, and she had corresponded incessantly with the Catholic continental powers to aid her cause. She wanted her freedom and her Scottish crown. She also probably wanted Elizabeth's throne. In August 1586 Walsingham uncovered a conspiracy to murder Elizabeth, and Mary was implicated. On November 29, after a dramatic trial in which the queen of the Scots conducted her own defense with great wit and courage, the English Parliament sentenced her to death.

James was presented with a considerable dilemma. How could his precious alliance (and stipend), not to mention his hope of succeeding Elizabeth, survive the execution of his mother? All the factions in Scotland, even Mary's old enemies, were united in resenting the offensive and humiliating English sentence. Maitland, now the chancellor, urged James to threaten the alliance, which the king did, but with little fervor. Gray was sent to London to save the king's mother, but another Scottish delegation secretly undermined his labors by

Reluctant to take the blame for Mary's death, and afraid that the Catholic powers of Europe would seek revenge, Elizabeth waited six weeks after Parliament's sentencing before signing Mary's death warrant in February 1587.

On the morning of February 8, 1587, Mary was taken to the executioner's block in the great hall at Fotheringay Castle. Her death posed a problem for James, who did not want to jeopardize his claim to the English throne by antagonizing Elizabeth.

letting Elizabeth know that James would "with tyme [time] digest the worst." James wanted to avoid bloodshed. Moreover, the English Parliament had passed an act in 1584 prohibiting the succession of anyone who took up arms in Mary's cause. If Scotland went to war for Mary, James could never be king of England. If Mary was saved, James's own rule in Scotland was in danger. The king made formal, feeble protests to the English. Mary was beheaded on February 8, 1587.

James blocked every effort to avenge his mother's death. When Lord Maxwell threatened to burn the northern English city of Newcastle, James sent him out of the country. The rash young earl of Bothwell, nephew of Mary's last husband, said the king's mourning clothes should be a suit of armor, but James kept the peace. Maitland accused the luckless Gray, who had failed to save Mary, of betraying her, and James allowed his favorite to fall, a convenient scapegoat. Soon after, the king let Elizabeth know that a contribution from England could help assuage his grief.

In the crisis following the trial and execution of Mary, James dealt with his wild, anarchic nobles in a novel way. On May 15, 1587, he called his peers to a great feast in Edinburgh. By royal command, all present had to toast each other and then walk up High Street, each man hand-in-hand with his greatest enemy. In this harmonious atmosphere, Maitland even managed to negotiate a truce between Crown and Kirk.

Under the splendid administration of Maitland, a centralization of authority in the Scottish Crown was occurring that resembled the transformation achieved in England a generation earlier. Maitland reorganized the uncertain Scottish courts and set up machinery to enforce their decrees. He levied new taxes. The taming of the Kirk left the crown in possession of vacant benefices that had previously been at the disposal of the hereditary nobles. The admission of lesser landholders, called "lairds," to the Scottish parliament further diminished the power of the lords, thus strengthening the Crown.

Reforms would not have been enough to quell the

Scottish nobles without a display of royal muscle, too. In 1589 the rising star at the court was a charming and subtle young man named George Gordon, earl of Huntly. Huntly was named captain of the king's guard and one of his men, Alexander Lindsay, was soon installed as the king's new bedfellow. Huntly and his circle were bitterly resentful, however, of the great power held by Maitland.

Queen Elizabeth spoiled Huntly's merry domination of the Scottish court when she sent James a packet of intercepted letters exposing the earl's part in a Catholic plan to invade England. "Pluck up treason by the roots," the angry queen instructed James. With great reluctance, James had his captain arrested but shortly thereafter set him free. This was too much for Maitland, who threatened to resign, so James banished Huntly from the court. Huntly, who charged that Maitland was controlling the king, roused the Highland clans. To everyone's great surprise, James was soon in arms himself, and he and Maitland led an army north from Edinburgh. On April 17, 1589, outside the city of Aberdeen at the Bridge of Dee, the armies converged, but no battle ensued. Some of the rebel troops had disappeared when they heard the king was in arms, and the rest now did the same. The victorious monarch, ever mindful that his authority depended on balancing all factions and destroying none, forgave the vanquished.

The king and his chancellor had been vigorous in establishing and defending the independent authority of the Stuart Crown, and they now turned their attention to preserving it for posterity. James had to secure the succession. The search for a royal bride was narrowed to two candidates: Catherine de Bourbon, sister of Henry of Navarre, the prospective heir to the throne of France; and Anne of Denmark, the younger daughter of King Frederick. The Frenchman, however, had no money for a dowry, and his sister, at 40, was said to be "old and crooked and somewhat worse if all were known." Princess Anne, on the other hand, was a beautiful, blonde, vivacious 15 year old, and her father could afford a fine dowry. Edinburgh and the rising mer-

King Philip II of Spain, shown with his wife, Queen Mary of England, was one of the most powerful Catholic lords of Europe. In his quest for the English crown, James sought the support of Spain, thus beginning a rocky, life-long alliance with that staunchly Catholic country.

chant class favored the Danish match; much of their trade was with the Protestant countries of the Baltic Sea. A rumor that Maitland opposed the Danish match caused a riot in the capital, and James could only calm the crowd by revealing that he had already chosen Anne.

Maitland tried to negotiate a good marriage treaty with the Danes, but James, suddenly grown unaccountably romantic, thwarted his efforts, declaring that he would not be a merchant for his bride. However, he could hardly afford to get married. The English ambassador speculated sadly that "Scotland was never in a worse state to receive a queen, for there is not a house in repair." Elizabeth grudgingly sent James some money, and a Scottish embassy sailed for Denmark. James and Anne were married by proxy in Copenhagen on August 20, 1589, but stormy weather kept the bride from crossing to her new home. The royal bridegroom chafed at the delay, writing sonnets and dreaming of his bride. When he learned that Anne was stranded in Oslo, he decided to prove to the whole world that he was "no irresolute ass who could do nothing of himself" and impulsively sailed off to get her. He took

James ruled Scotland ably and vigorously. He shrewdly balanced all the conflicting factions, thus strengthening his own authority while checking the power of the Protestant nobles, the Kirk, and the Catholic lords.

On August 28, 1589, James married pretty, 15-year-old Anne of Denmark by proxy. James impulsively traveled to Norway to intercept the queen on her way to Scotland, and the couple held a lavish wedding celebration in Oslo.

Maitland with him, but he cleverly left behind two rival councils to keep each other in check.

The expedition reached Norway in five days, made the 200-mile trek to Oslo, and celebrated a great state wedding on November 23. In the ensuing festivities, James distinguished himself by his ability to drink deep and even accepted an invitation to continue the party in Copenhagen. He was out of Scotland for six months. James listened to long speeches, went riding, visited with the Danish royal family at Kronberg Castle in Elsinore, debated in Latin with learned theologians, and discussed the new Copernican theory with the great astronomer Tycho Brahe at his observatory on the island of Hveen. The king seemed very much in love with his new bride, and he was having a marvelous time. Affairs in Scotland, however, would soon recall James to the demanding realities of a king's life.

4

A Waiting Game

James had left his factions — the independent Highland Catholic lords, the unruly Protestant border lords, and the quarrelsome Kirk — cunningly balanced. But he returned from Denmark on May 1, 1590, to find various groups strong enough to challenge him. The first test came from the Kirk. James had decided that Anne would be anointed with holy oil at her coronation, and the Kirk was outraged. James prevailed—Anne was anointed and crowned in an elaborate seven-hour ceremony on May 17—but the Kirk was not conquered.

The second challenge was more serious. Wild, dangerous, and ambitious Francis Hepburn, the handsome young earl of Bothwell, was a Protestant and a popular man with the Kirk. A strong border lord, he had been popular with James, too, at first, but his arrogance and independence had brought the king to hate and fear him. In addition, James believed that Bothwell was a professed sorcerer who had attempted to use black magic to harm him.

The Protestant reformers who helped break the old power of the Catholic church had opened the way for a surge of interest in satanic cults and in the mysterious practice of witchcraft. Witches were persecuted all over Europe, and James took a very strong interest in the trials held in Scotland. He

> *He is patient in the work of government, makes no decision without obtaining good counsel and is said to be one of the most secret princes of the world.*
> —HENRY WOTTON
> English diplomat, on King James in Scotland

Despite numerous challenges by the Scottish nobles and the insistent interference in government by the Protestant church, James always asserted that his royal power was divine and absolute. He wrote two treatises expressing his absolutist beliefs, *The Trew Law of Free Monarchies* and *Basilikon Doron* .

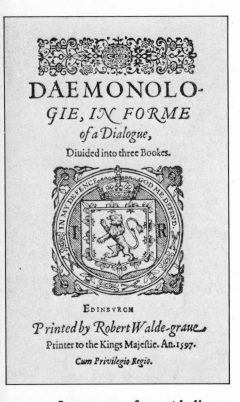

DAEMONOLO-
GIE, IN FORME
of a Dialogue,
Diuided into three Bookes.

EDINBVRGH
Printed by Robert Walde-graue
Printer to the Kings Majestie. An. 1597.
Cum Privilegio Regio.

James was a fervent believer
in the powers of witchcraft
and published a book on the
subject, entitled *Daemonologie*, in 1597. English playwright William Shakespeare
is said to have borrowed ma-
terial from James's book for
his play *Macbeth*.

attended the questioning and torture of witnesses, asking occasional questions and even suggesting new methods of getting at the truth. He wrote a vivid account of the subject, *Daemonologie*, which was published in 1597. While he was sailing to Denmark, witches had tied live cats to the severed joints of dead bodies and cast them into the sea to raise storms to drown him. They had also passed a little wax image around a circle with these words: "This is King James the Sixth, ordained to be consumed at the instance of a nobleman, Francis, earl of Bothwell."

Bothwell, known as "the Wizard Earl," was arrested and charged with witchcraft and treason in April 1591, but his stature and the support of the Kirk kept him from trial. In June he escaped, and the king declared him an outlaw, seizing his estates. On December 27, Bothwell and his men broke into Holyrood Palace, but James escaped into a tower and stood off the assault until help came from Edinburgh. Bothwell got away, but nine of his men were hanged the following day. In January 1592 James heard that Bothwell was nearby and rode off in pursuit, but the adventure ended badly: James fell off his horse into the icy Tyne River.

The king's continuing difficulties with the Wizard Earl were interrupted by a brief but bloody incident. Huntly, the leader of the Catholic lords, was the most powerful man at court. All the gentlemen of the bedchamber and the stable, the men closest to the king on a day-to-day basis, were Huntly's men. On February 7, 1592, Huntly attacked the castle of Donibristle to get at his enemy, the handsome and debonair James Stewart, second earl of Moray (the son-in-law of Mary's brother), a great supporter of the Kirk and an ally of Bothwell's. The castle was set on fire, and as Moray fled, Huntly struck the death blow, a nasty cut across the face. The slaying caused a great outcry against the Catholics, but James took no action and let Huntly slip away. Elizabeth was so angry at his reluctance to punish the lawless Catholics that she reduced his pension, but James may not have been sorry to see a strong ally of Bothwell's fall, and he had neither the power nor the will to curb his Highland friends.

The factions that swirled around the court had drawn in another unusual plotter, the vivacious and extravagant queen. Anne had taken a strong dislike to the meddling Kirk and to the sober chancellor as well, and she showed increasing favor to the glamorous Catholic lords. At some point in these early years of her marriage, Anne actually converted to Catholicism. This nearly unbearable insult to the Kirk may actually have aided the king in his unending struggle to secure his rule by balancing factions. For all the reported friction caused by Anne's conversion and other sporadic domestic problems, James always treated his queen with forbearance. Their marriage was harmonious enough to produce seven children, though only three would live to be adults.

Blame for the murder of Moray and the refusal to pursue the murderers were centered finally on the power behind the throne, Maitland, who was widely believed to have his eye on some of Moray's lands. Maitland was forced by his opponents to retire from the court, though not from the king's service, in March 1592. Two months later his careful policies were still bearing fruit. James summoned a parliament in May that softened the "black acts" of 1584 with new "golden acts," which confirmed the authority of the ministers in ecclesiastical matters and moved James closer to the weakened Kirk.

On June 27 the Wizard Earl led a large group of armed men in a siege of the king's palace of Falkland, at Fife. Bothwell's plan — certainly not a new one in James's turbulent history — was to rule the country by capturing the king. When the attack failed, the rebel escaped to England, but Bothwell's departure did not ensure a tranquil Scotland.

In December the Catholic lords put the king at the center of an international crisis. A Scottish Catholic named George Kerr was arrested carrying detailed plans of a Spanish plot to land an army in Scotland and then invade England. Kerr also carried blank pages signed and sealed by Huntly and his

To ensure that Scotland did not become too powerful, Queen Elizabeth preferred to keep her northern neighbor in a constant state of confusion. She meddled in the conflict between the Scottish Protestants and Catholics and aided some of James's most powerful dissident lords, much to the king's distress.

43

friends. These "blanks" would allow the king of Spain to fill in whatever treacherous commitments he desired from the reckless Highlanders. Besides the incriminating "Spanish blanks," Kerr's packet contained a typically wishy-washy memo from James about the advantages and disadvantages of a Spanish invasion.

The revelations galvanized the Kirk and Queen Elizabeth, though they were hardly natural allies; Elizabeth's High Commission persecuted reforming Protestants more vigorously than English Catholics. However, James declared that no prosecution of the Catholic lords would be possible. He had made up his mind to strike at Bothwell before he dealt with the Catholics.

He got his chance sooner than he expected. He was still in his nightgown at Holyrood on the morning of July 24, 1593, when he was suddenly confronted by the Wizard Earl. Bothwell knelt and laid his sword on the floor before him. James tried to escape, but Bothwell caught him. He said the king could take the sword and slay him or accept his faithful service. Having no desire to kill anybody personally, James was forced to "forgive" the man he had so recently outlawed, and Bothwell and his allies took up positions of power at the court. A royal proclamation restored Bothwell's lands, and his trial for witchcraft proceeded to an expected acquittal.

Bothwell's arrogance made enemies even of the Protestant lords who were his natural allies. James soon fled to Stirling Castle, where he was joined by Bothwell's opponents, and he announced that his peace with the Wizard Earl had been coerced. Bothwell was outlawed again and forbidden to come near the court.

In September the Catholic lords were excommunicated by the Kirk. When James promised the Catholics a fair trial, the Kirkmen were enraged. Passions were high enough to threaten a civil war, but Maitland eased the crisis by moving a compromise Act of Abolition through the parliament. It stipulated that the Presbyterianism of the Kirk would be the only faith allowed in Scotland. Those

> [Bothwell's] behavior would have tried the peace of mind of a far more stable and courageous personality than James. In addition, it must be remembered that James was without a standing army of any sort . . . [and was] at the mercy of any rebellious noble who was the fortunate possessor of the loyal band that James lacked.
>
> —ANTONIA FRASER
> English biographer, on James's conflict with the earl of Bothwell

who refused to accept the official religion by January 1, 1594, would have to leave the country. They would not, however, have to forfeit their properties or revenues. Maitland's compromise pleased no one, but it managed to restore some calm.

Scotland had a rare respite from these broils on January 19, 1594, when the king's first child, a son, was born at Stirling Castle. He was named Henry, and the rejoicing at his birth was so great, a witness commented that the people of Scotland seemed "daft for mirth." James made elaborate plans for the christening in August, but the fragile domestic peace broke apart again.

The Protestant ministers thundered against the Act of Abolition. They did not want the Catholic lords to get away with their fortunes intact and stir up trouble all over Europe. For their part, the Catholic Highlanders did not care to choose between the Kirk and exile. As tempers rose again, Elizabeth made a typically devious decision to strike at the Catholics by giving Bothwell some support, and the Wizard Earl came home prepared to fight. James went to the Kirk and begged the citizens of Edinburgh for help. He made a stern promise: If the Kirk would help him crush Bothwell, he would drive Huntly and his friends out of Scotland. At the Battle

Stirling Castle, set atop a high hill, was one of the royal strongholds in Scotland. Just as James had been sent there as a baby for safety, in 1595 he ordered that his firstborn son and heir, Prince Henry, remain under care at Stirling.

of Niddrie, though the king himself ran away, the royal forces triumphed — but the Wizard Earl escaped.

James celebrated Prince Henry's christening on August 30 with jousting, pageantry, and feasting. The king then set about to keep his promise. Elizabeth even sent money to help root out the Catholics. The royal forces, under Archibald Campbell, earl of Argyll, were defeated by the Catholics at Glenlivet on October 3, but the victory cost the rebels too many men. Huntly fled, and James, following closely behind, spoiled his castle at Strathbogie. In March 1595, outlawed and beggared by the victorious king, Huntly left Scotland. The following month the Wizard Earl skulked off as well. James had broken the power of the Highlands and the border, and six years of relative peace ensued.

James's crown had never been so secure, nor so resplendent. In the summer of 1595, in order to make the throne less vulnerable to the old game of kidnapping, he sent Prince Henry to be cared for by the earl of Mar in the stronghold of Stirling. Queen Anne fought being separated from her baby, but James insisted. He knew the lesson it had cost his mother so much grief to learn: Whoever held the heir controlled the crown. Though Anne protested bitterly, the baby prince went off to his guardian.

When Maitland died in October, the king resolved to let no other adviser attain such power. He would henceforth be served, he said, only by men that he "might convict and were hangable." He celebrated his new independence in a series of moves designed to bring the country more law and order. Proclaiming his absolute authority, he shored up the courts and cracked down on the bloody private feuds so common in Scotland. He sent settlers in an attempt to civilize the wild Western Isles (the Hebrides, off the northwest coast of Scotland), and he negotiated with Elizabeth a joint commission to tame the lawless border region.

In January 1596, more than usually nipped by his chronic poverty, James appointed councilors to manage his budget and revenues. These eight men, known as the Octavians, instituted some useful reforms, but some of the men were Catholics and their appointment riled the Kirk. In August James's second child was born. He named her Elizabeth; her sole godparent was the English queen for whom she was named.

Later in the year, the Catholic crisis worsened. James decided to allow Huntly and his friends to return to Scotland if they would accept the faith of the Kirk. When an Edinburgh preacher said that Satan ruled in the royal court and that all kings were children of the devil, James angrily demanded satisfaction for the insult. The ministers defied him, and the people, stirred up by rebellious sermons, rioted. James's response was superb: He moved the court to Linlithgow. Faced with certain ruin, the people of Edinburgh chased the offending

In August 1600 a bizarre incident took place when James was abducted while at Gowrie House by the earl of Gowrie. Despite their declaration of innocence, Gowrie and his brother were attacked and slain by the king's men while the king (far right) looked on in horror.

preachers out of town and welcomed back the king. Moderates replaced the firebrands in the Kirk.

During this time James set down his views on kingship for the edification of posterity. His long pamphlet, *The Trew Law of Free Monarchies*, published anonymously in 1598, advocated the doctrine of the divine right of kings and instructed the people in their duties toward their God-given monarch. A longer book, *Basilikon Doron*, written specifically to instruct Prince Henry in the rights and duties of kingship, was published a year later. Substantially culled from other Renaissance treatises on the education of princes, James's book has a vigorous and lively style and a wealth of personal anecdote and observation. It was a best-seller in its time and still gives James his main claim to literary accomplishment. Advising his son on matters of dress and table manners, as well as moral behavior and statecraft, James manages to be pompous, witty, frank, and touching all at once. He recommends, for example, that the prince should always wear armor when going into battle, unless he wants to be light enough "for away running," a tactic he knew well.

A mysterious incident occurred in August 1600, the only account of which comes from the king. It is too bizarre, with too many inconsistencies and improbabilities, to be taken on faith. James was hunting one morning when 19-year-old Alexander, master of Ruthven, invited him to Gowrie House with a confused story about a strange visitor and a pot of gold. At Gowrie House, James was received by Ruthven's brother, the 22-year-old earl of Gowrie. After an impromptu dinner, Ruthven took the king off—unattended—to see the visitor. Some time later James appeared at a tower window overlooking the courtyard and shrieked for help. When his courtiers rushed to save him, they found Ruthven on his knees, clutching the king and covering his mouth as if to keep him from crying out. Though Ruthven pleaded his innocence, the king's men quickly cut him down. When his brother came running to see what had happened, they killed him, too. James knelt immediately and gave thanks for his "deliv-

Kings exercise a manner or resemblance of Divine power upon earth. They can make or unmake their subjects: they have a power of life and death; judges over all their subjects and in all causes, and yet accountable to God only.
—KING JAMES I

erance." The bodies of the slain were stripped, quartered, and hung on the walls as a warning to all traitors. The family properties reverted to the king, and the 80,000 pounds James owed the earl was effectively canceled.

No one could figure out, then or since, what really happened. The Gowrie family, which was known to have dabbled in both witchcraft and treason, did have some reason to be at odds with the king. But if the Gowries were trying to kidnap or murder James at Gowrie House, they could hardly have planned worse or acted more ineptly. On the other hand, it was known very well that the king was a coward. If he had set out to destroy these young men, he could have taken steps that would not have exposed him to physical danger.

Five ministers of Edinburgh refused to obey the king's command to tell his story and proclaim his innocence from their pulpits, but the weakened Kirk could not stand against the emphatic crown. Other ministers were appointed, and four of the rebels complied. The only one who maintained his skepticism was driven out of Scotland. In the wider world, though, skepticism prevailed. In England and France, the story of James's miraculous escape was greeted with laughter and mockery.

During this time, the obsession to inherit Elizabeth's crown dominated James's actions, and his attempts to present himself as the authentic Protestant heir while maintaining his appeal to the English Catholics nearly got him into serious trouble several times when factions sought his support to lend legitimacy to their plotting. The most tempting of all the conspiracies was the strange plot fomented by Robert Devereux, earl of Essex, who led an abortive coup in February 1601 against Elizabeth. He planned to set James on the English throne, and it was clear that James had been corresponding with him, but the men around Elizabeth managed to keep his name out of the trial. Essex was found guilty of treason and beheaded. James was grateful that his prospects had survived but lamented the loss of a strong supporter.

Queen Elizabeth delivers a resounding box on the ear to the arrogant earl of Essex, Robert Devereux. Essex had been a favorite of the queen, but in 1601 he led a conspiracy to remove Elizabeth and install James on the English throne.

49

As James cast about for some new strategy to gain the English throne, the most powerful and efficient of Elizabeth's ministers, the dapper, hunchbacked Robert Cecil, secretly came forward to teach him the virtue of patience. In an elaborately coded and circuitous correspondence that Elizabeth surely would have regarded as treason, Cecil assured James of his strong support. Cecil knew that James had the strongest claim to inherit the crown, the country would accept him, and he already had two sons to ensure the succession (Prince Charles was born in 1600). By careful flattery and manipulation, the crafty Cecil instructed James in how to deal with Elizabeth. James's letters stopped whining and nagging and became so agreeably sunny and flattering that the queen even complimented him on the change.

Robert Cecil, earl of Salisbury, was one of Elizabeth's most powerful advisers. A skillful politician, he was instrumental in securing James's accession to the English throne.

Queen Elizabeth died on March 24, 1602, surrounded by the members of her privy council, who interpreted her last gestures to mean that she wanted James to succeed her on the throne.

Queen Elizabeth died on March 24, 1603. Her privy council, led by Cecil, gathered at the deathbed and later reported that she indicated her desire to have James succeed her. Whether or not that was the case, James was clearly the choice of the council, which proclaimed him king that same afternoon. Official notice was sent to Edinburgh to inform James that he was now also king of England, France, and Ireland. (The traditional title for the English monarch referred to ancient French territories England no longer held.) A man close to James was asked how he thought the king would greet the news. He answered, "Even, my lord, like a poor man that hath been wandering in the wilderness for forty years and hath at last come within sight of the Land of Promise."

REGERE IMPERIO POPULOS

JAMES I.
KING of GREAT BRITAIN
FRANCE and IRELAND
Defender of the Faith &c.

5

The Promised Land

On April 5, 1603, the new "King of Great Britain," as he decided to call himself, bade farewell to his melancholy northern capital and began an extraordinary journey south to his glorious new capital, London. He had managed to hold on in Scotland for 37 years, but now he made the disastrous mistake of viewing England as his reward. He saw himself as God's anointed — an absolute king — and he expected to be treated as such.

As his court moved away from Edinburgh, every Scot who could manage it got attached to the king's retinue. At the same time, huge numbers of Englishmen flocked north to greet him. After the deprivations of his childhood and the straitened circumstances of his adult life, James was radiant with joy at all the extravagance and flattery. At Berwick, on the long-disputed border, he received the people's cheers and a purse of gold. In Newcastle, he granted an amnesty for most of the prisoners. At York he met with Robert Cecil to discuss his upcoming coronation. He told Cecil he required more money; he had had barely enough to bring his retinue out of Scotland, and expenses were rising. James rewarded Cecil by agreeing to dismiss Sir Walter Raleigh, Cecil's old enemy, from his post as captain of the Queen's Guard.

However high his hopes, James's real legacy was a Crown weakened by inflation and by the costs of war with Spain, a government undermined by faction and an administration polluted by corruption.
—MENNA PRESTWICH
British historian, on state of England at the time of James's accession

Upon the death of Elizabeth, England and Scotland were united under James, king of Great Britain. Although the inscription on this portrait adds the phrase "Defender of the Faith," James was by temperament opposed to harsh persecution of the minority Catholics in England.

At Durham, Bishop Tobias Matthew introduced James to his bishops, the learned and deferential princes of the English church, of which James was now the head. James enjoyed discussing theology with these agreeable men, who were so different from the stubborn Scottish Kirkmen, and the warm feelings that sprang up that night between king and bishops would last a lifetime.

Not everything that happened on the progress (royal state journey) was happy. At Newark-upon-Trent a pickpocket was captured, and the king ordered him hanged without a trial. Such an arbitrary response may have been common in lawless Scotland, but in England, there were courts and justices to deal with crime. James had a lot to learn about the laws and rights of Englishmen.

As the court continued its journey, James was dazzled by the wealth of England. After the financial constraints he had suffered, he was eager to believe that he had come into unlimited riches. So many people came to see the king that they injured each other in the commotion. So many nobles vied for honors that one witness described the process "as if it were first come, first served, or that preferment were a goal to be got by footmanship." Francis Bacon, one of the finest writers in an age of great writing, referred to "this almost prostituted title of knighthood" in the very letter he wrote asking his cousin Cecil to get one for him. Knighting men became so common that once, James forgot the name

Westminster Abbey, which looks out onto the Thames River, has been the site of English coronations since William the Conqueror's in 1066. Much of the present structure — with its high arching vaults and flying buttresses — was built by King Henry VIII in the mid-16th century.

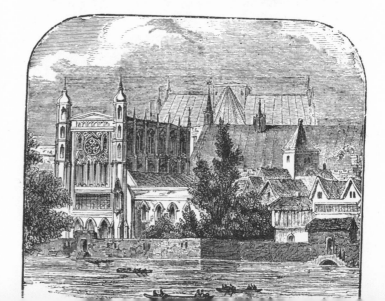

of the man he was dubbing and told him, "Prithee, rise up, and call thyself Sir What-Thou-Wilt."

Almost lost in the excitement was an event that would prove to be of immense importance. A group of church reformers loosely referred to as Puritans politely presented to the king a document called the Millenary Petition, a moderate, articulate list of grievances and suggestions for reform reportedly signed by a thousand ministers. The Puritans were characterized by an absolute hostility to Rome, a deep desire to be united with the Protestant churches of Europe, and a great strictness in matters of doctrine and ceremony, with a strong emphasis on independent Bible reading and on preaching. Some reforms seemed necessary: Half the English clergy were desperately poor; most had no college degrees and were not even licensed to preach. Pluralism, the practice of one minister holding multiple offices and farming out his livings at starvation wages, was widespread.

James mistakenly associated the well-educated, thoughtful Puritans with those other reformers he knew so well — the haughty, fanatical Kirkmen. The Millenary Petition, however, was no fiery call for radical change. It asked for a simplified church ceremony, an end to pluralism, the raising of stipends to attract better preachers to the church, and a stricter observance of the Sabbath. James received the petition graciously; he loved being an arbiter, especially of great theological questions, and he had supreme confidence in his abilities. He expected to restore universal harmony, and to that end he resolved to call a great religious conference. This response encouraged the Puritans, but it also inspired additional, less moderate, petitions. The well-bred, wealthy bishops warned James that what the Puritans really wanted was "the utter overthrow" of the English church.

On May 3, at Theobalds, Cecil's splendid country estate, James met the rest of Elizabeth's privy council. It would be his council too, of course, with the addition of several Scots (including the earl of Mar, his son's guardian, and the duke of Lennox, Esmé

On April 5, 1603, James began his journey south to assume the throne of England. An enormous retinue accompanied him, and the new king was joyously received throughout the country.

Stuart's son) and other Englishmen. The outbreak of plague in London postponed the king's triumphal entry, but he managed to slip into the capital to have a look at the crown jewels. James had taken to wearing extra layers of clothing to protect against an assassin's dagger. He had always been afraid, with good reason, of any Scottish crowd, and he now grew tired of the hordes of people constantly clamoring to see him. He slipped away for two months of hunting.

The coronation ceremony, greatly reduced because of the plague, took place on July 25, 1603. The attending lords held handkerchiefs over their mouths to protect against contagion, and Anne embarrassed James by refusing the Anglican communion. Anne's Catholicism had been helpful in balancing Scottish factions, but the English were suspicious of the Catholic queen. Indeed, the situation of English Catholics was precarious. They were not free to practice their religion openly. The government levied stiff fines on "recusants," those who did not attend Anglican services. In practice, the recusancy fines were aimed primarily at Catholics. James had held out a promise of toleration to gain the support of English Catholics, but he had also promised no toleration to win over the English Protestants. His own preference was for toleration, but Cecil explained to him that the Crown needed the revenue from the fines, and James agreed to continue the persecution.

James's broken promise to the English Catholics caused trouble even before the coronation. An angry priest named William Watson plotted to kidnap the king at Greenwich to force him to declare a policy of toleration. This foolish and ill-considered "Bye Plot" was revealed and quickly suppressed, but the investigation that followed uncovered a more dangerous plot to depose James and replace him with his English cousin, Lady Arabella Stuart (who knew nothing of the matter). Sir Walter Raleigh, falsely implicated in this "Main Plot," was subjected to a

King James I of England and Queen Anne were crowned on July 25, 1603, at Westminster Abbey. Anne embarrassed James by refusing to accept an Anglican communion, and James was forced to kneel alone before the archbishop of Canterbury.

disgraceful show trial conducted by Sir Edward Coke, an eminent jurist. Raleigh was charged with conspiring to bring Spanish troops into England. Despite the lack of solid evidence against him, he was convicted. Father Watson and the conspirators in the Bye Plot were cruelly executed, but James spared the principles in the Main Plot. On December 15, 1603, Raleigh was taken to the Tower of London, where he would spend the next 13 years.

James's reaction to the Catholic plots was odd but typical. He suspended the recusancy fines and allowed Catholics to worship freely. Such tolerance may have alarmed many around the king, but it must have pleased the queen. At Christmas 1603, with plots and plague behind it, the court began to relax. Anne's passion for rich clothes, jewels, dancing, and merrymaking set the tone. It was a playful,

Lady Arabella Stuart was the daughter of Lord Darnley's younger brother, Charles Stuart, and thus a potential heir to the English throne. In 1603 a plot was discovered to overthrow James, install his cousin Arabella as queen, and restore Catholicism to England.

amorous court, with lavish feasting and considerable drinking. Anne had a particular fondness for masques, elaborate affairs that historian G. P. V. Akrigg described as "part masquerade ball, part drama, and part pure pageantry." Under King James, the masters of the masque were Ben Jonson and Inigo Jones. Poet and playwright Jonson set the themes and wrote the dramatic scenes. Architect and painter Jones designed the splendid costumes and set the magnificent stages that were the wonders of the court.

The long Christmas revel at Hampton Court was hardly over when the king summoned his bishops and the Puritan leaders and on January 14, 1604, opened the Hampton Court Conference to resolve the questions that had been raised by the Millenary Petition. His desire to show off his wide learning, his dream of restoring religious harmony, and his conviction that he alone had the power to dictate policy to English clergymen all led him to undertake this unfortunate action.

On the first day of the conference, James consulted with his bishops alone. They were led by John Whitgift, the archbishop of Canterbury, and Richard Bancroft, the severe, mean-spirited bishop of London. Wearing their rich robes and tall miters, the conservative churchmen marveled as their monarch orated and disputed with obvious glee. On the second day, the learned Puritans, led by Dr. John Reynolds of Oxford, were allowed to join the conference. They, too, marveled at their monarch, but not for the same reason. James, who still thought of them as English Kirkmen, was rude and abusive, siding with the bishops on most disputed points of doctrine and church government. When the Puritans resisted, it infuriated him. "I will make them conform themselves or I will harry them out of this land or else do worse," he threatened. Bancroft provided James with a list of articles of faith to which the Puritans objected, and James directed them to conform or lose their ministries.

James considered the Hampton Court Conference a great success and bragged about how he had "pep-

Inigo Jones was the founder of the English classical school of architecture. In addition to designing several royal structures, including the great Banqueting House at Whitehall, Jones was responsible for the fanciful costumes and elaborate stage sets of the court masques that were Queen Anne's favorite amusement.

pered" the Puritans. The bishops were also pleased. In truth, however, the conference was a disaster. James's arrogant, patronizing, deeply offensive treatment of the Puritans only alienated them and made them more defiant. Perhaps as many as 90 Puritan ministers lost their positions. With some of the best men driven out of the Church of England, the church itself became more rigid and intolerant.

In fact the only real success of the conference — and the greatest triumph of the reign — was a Puritan initiative for a new translation of the Bible. James set 54 translators to work and oddly enough, Dr. Reynolds, the Puritan leader, was among them. James wanted a clear, straightforward English Bi-

Ben Jonson was Inigo Jones's partner in the staging of court revelries. He wrote the dramatic scenes for eight court masques performed between 1605 and 1612. Jonson was also a gifted poet and playwright whose works greatly influenced Jacobean theater.

ble, and he played an active part in overseeing the work. The King James Version, first published in 1611, remains a vital masterpiece from the great age of English prose.

James went from his religious disaster at Hampton Court to a parliamentary disaster at Westminster. Even before Parliament met, the king issued a proclamation showing his fundamental ignorance of English law and parliamentary custom. He declared that any disputed elections, normally decided by Parliament, would now be resolved by his own court of chancery. Thus began the long, bitter battle the Stuart kings would have with the increasingly powerful Parliament.

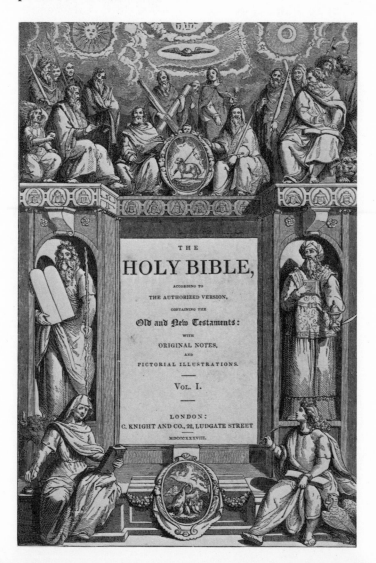

In an effort to reconcile religious conflicts, James summoned the Hampton Court Conference in 1604. The meeting was a disaster, but one valuable proposal came out of it: the commissioning of a new translation of the Bible. The resulting *King James Version*, printed in 1611, remains a testament to the splendor of the English language.

On March 19, 1604, James opened Parliament with a speech that contained some farsighted ideas, including his dream of Anglo-Scottish union and his desire to end the long war with Spain, but his arrogance and confrontational style alienated many of the representatives. He began by congratulating the members on "the blessings which God hath in my person bestowed upon you all." The first action of the defiant body, however, was to throw out a chancery verdict in an election dispute. James was furious and declared that all parliamentary privileges depended on his good will, but in the end he backed down. The members hesitantly agreed to set up a commission to consider the effects of union with Scotland, but they had serious misgivings about a Spanish peace. England had been at war with Catholic Spain for two decades and had long been supporting the Dutch Protestants, who were rebelling against Spanish rule. Concluding peace with Spain would mean abandoning the Dutch.

In dealing with Parliament, James made a fundamental error of judgment; the body that he faced in England was not the powerless, anarchic gaggle of factions he had known in Scotland. King Henry VIII had strengthened the English Parliament in order to free the Crown from the nobles and the Catholic church, and Parliament guarded its privileges jealously.

James's mistreatment of the Puritans at Hampton Court had resulted in the swift election to Parliament of many Puritan leaders. In June 1604 the Commons, the elected house of Parliament, drafted the remarkable "Apology and Satisfaction" to correct the king's "misinformations," which had "seriously and dangerously impugned" not only the privileges of Parliament but "the liberties and stability of the whole kingdom." Parliamentary privileges were not held at the pleasure of an absolute king, it declared, but as "a right and due inheritance." The Apology also upheld the traditional liberties of Englishmen. This bold document was never formally presented to James, but it was clear he had read a copy when he petulantly rebuked the house at its closing session in July.

Whatever bad impressions of James the members took with them on their recess were quickly compounded when Convocation, the council of English bishops, passed 104 new canons, or church laws. The Apology had specifically denied Convocation any power to make new laws without the consent of Parliament. Nevertheless, James attempted to legitimize the canons when he proclaimed that all ministers had until November 30 to conform to the new laws or lose their posts. The enforcement of religious conformity ultimately caused the emigration of a number of English Puritans. Seeking the freedom to worship as they chose, they went first to Holland. Some then crossed the Atlantic, headed for the fledgling English colony in Virginia, but their ship, the *Mayflower*, went off course, and in December 1620 they landed at what is now Plymouth, Massachusetts. With the help of the local Indians, they began to scrape a living from the harsh New World.

For many Englishmen, the bloom was off the Stuart rose, and James was no longer so chirpy about "the promised land." He began to leave the details of government to Cecil, now earl of Salisbury, and the privy council so he could spend more time hunting. The king's great passion had its peculiar aspects. He would gallop frantically after the

Hunting was James's passion, and one traditional technique was hawking. This royal sport used trained falcons to hunt small game and was much less disruptive to the countryside than James's deer-hunting escapades.

hounds, leap off his horse to cut the deer's throat, bathe his arms in its blood, and then smear it on the faces of his most favored companions. He liked all the blood sports popular in his day: cock fighting, bear baiting, and bull baiting. He collected animals and boasted a zoo of crocodiles, camels, an elephant, a tiger, and a flying squirrel from Virginia.

James was less pleased with another novelty brought from America. In 1604 he wrote a pamphlet, *A Counterblaste to Tobacco*, a strikingly modern attack on the nasty habit Raleigh had brought back from the New World. Many Englishmen were already addicted: There were 7,000 tobacco shops in James's London. Published anonymously, the pamphlet stated that smoking was "loathsome to the eye, hateful to the nose, harmful to the brain, dangerous to the lungs." Any nonsmoker married to a smoker, James wrote, would either have to take up smoking or "resolve to live in a perpetual stinking torment."

James's hunting put a severe burden on the countryside, which was required to sell the royal party whatever provisions, called purveyances, it needed at artificially low rates. In addition, the chaotic chase frequently destroyed the crops in the fields. In 1604 the people made a touching protest. One of James's hounds, Jowler, missing all day, came back with a letter tied around his neck. "Good Mr. Jowler," it read, "we pray you speak to the king (for he hears you every day and so doth he not us) that it will please his Majesty to go back to London, for else the country will be undone; all our provision is spent already and we are not able to entertain him." James was much amused by the letter, but stayed in the neighborhood another two weeks.

While the king hunted, the council did his bidding. In August 1604 Salisbury's hard work made one of James's dreams, peace with Spain, a reality. The fortunes of Spain had fallen off considerably after its great fleet, the Armada, met a sound defeat by Elizabeth's navy in 1588. Philip III now ruled an empire diminished by English piracy and the long war of attrition with the Dutch. James withdrew

> *His devotion to his sport [hunting] meant much inconvenience for his ministers. Foreign ambassadors had to be kept waiting, and necessary public business held in obeyance, until the King would reluctantly come back and meet with his Privy Council.*
>
> —G. P. V. AKRIGG
> Canadian historian, on
> James's passion for
> hunting

the letters of marque, documents that officially commissioned private citizens to prey as pirates on Spanish shipping. Then he had Salisbury hammer out the Treaty of 1604, which ended hostilities and opened the European part of the Spanish Empire (its American colonies were still off limits) to English trade. The treaty, however, still permitted the raising of volunteers in England to help the Dutch.

Peace with Spain was only the first step in James's grand design. His next vision was to preside over a great religious reconciliation, as Catholic and Puritan resolved their differences under the aegis of the moderate, welcoming Church of England. But the English people hated Spain and feared the reinstatement of Catholicism in England. James tried to ease their growing concern by changing his policy. He ordered a crackdown on the Catholics, who felt betrayed; many had only gradually revealed the secret of their faith because of the king's policy of toleration. However, James (and most of England)

As a result of Salisbury's hard work, English and Spanish statesmen met in London in 1604 to sign a treaty ending England's war with Spain. A delighted James then had Salisbury (lower right) negotiate English trading rights in Spain's European territories.

had been startled at the large number of once secret Catholics who had begun worshiping publicly. In this charged atmosphere occurred one of the most famous incidents in English history.

In May 1604 five bitter and resolute men, led by a Catholic gentleman named Robert Catesby, planted 36 barrels of gunpowder under the parliament building. They planned to ignite the explosive on opening day, when the royal family, privy council, bishops, and most of the country's leaders would be there. The conspiracy widened when the plotters decided to kidnap the king's daughter, Elizabeth, and effect a Catholic coup, with the young princess under a Catholic regency. Some of the men involved, however, felt uneasy at the thought of the unsuspecting Catholic lords who would perish in the explosion, and a man named Francis Tresham gave away the plot. He warned Lord Monteagle, his brother-in-law, with a mysterious letter, urging him to stay away from Parliament, because "they shall

James (seated, right) and his council interrogate Guy Fawkes regarding his part in the Gunpowder Plot. In May 1604, a group of disaffected Catholics planted 36 barrels of gunpowder under Parliament in an attempt to blow up James, the royal family, and the Protestant lords.

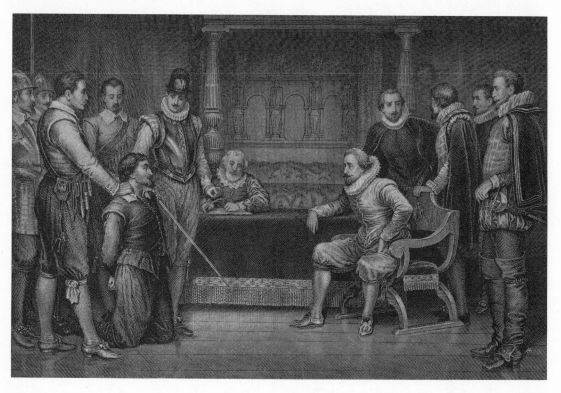

receive a terrible blow this Parliament, and yet they shall not see who hurts them." According to the official story, Lord Monteagle delivered the letter to Salisbury, who said he could not puzzle out the warning by himself. King James, however, immediately understood the oblique reference to gunpowder because of the circumstances of his father's death at Kirk o' Field.

On November 4, the day before the scheduled opening, Thomas Howard, lord chancellor and earl of Suffolk, conducted a thorough search of the building and discovered the gunpowder in the cellar. It was being guarded by a blunt soldier hardened in the Dutch wars, Guy Fawkes. When Fawkes was arrested, he declared that he was not sorry for the plot. "A dangerous disease requires a desperate remedy," he said. On November 9, James made a speech to Parliament, pointing out how lucky England was that nothing had happened to him. Kings had "sparkles of divinity," he said. He also added that not all English Catholics should be blamed for the work of a few fanatics. England rejoiced at the king's deliverance, and people lit bonfires across the land. (Every November 5, England continues to celebrate "Guy Fawkes Day," at which bonfires are lit and many "Guys" are burned in effigy.)

The conspirators were arrested, tortured, tried, and executed, with great cruelty, in the winter of 1606. England, more frightened of Catholicism than ever, drew closer to its peculiar king, and not a moment too soon, as far as James was concerned. In the two short years he had been king, he had fought major battles with the Puritans and Parliament, and he had survived three increasingly violent plots. England was proving less like the promised land and more like Scotland than this Lord's anointed had expected.

> *The Gunpowder Plot changed everything. The King, by nature neurotically fearful, had received a scare which he would not soon forget. So, for that matter, had England.*
> —G. P. V. AKRIGG
> Canadian historian, on the wave of anti-Catholic sentiment following the Gunpowder Plot

6
A Tarnished Crown

In Scotland, James had learned to balance factions to his own advantage. When he came to England, however, he forswore compromise and asserted himself as an absolute king. He offended everyone except the Anglican bishops and the court favorites who drew their power directly from him. He revealed himself to be pompous, arrogant, and extravagant. Unlike Elizabeth, the new king did not like contact with the common people. He did not relish the finer points of ceremony that had made his predecessor's court seem so magnificent.

James asserted himself as God's gift to the English, a position bound to raise hackles in the Commons. He told his first Parliament that God had made Scotland "to enjoy my birth and the first and most imperfect half of my life and you here [in England] to enjoy the perfect and last half thereof." The six years following the Gunpowder Plot should have been good years — they were uneventful and prosperous — but James continued to press conflicts that inevitably led to bitter conclusions.

In 1606, grateful for James's deliverance, Parliament voted him a large four-year subsidy despite royal expenditures far surpassing the king's income and widespread resentment at his extravagance in masques, jewels, and gifts to favorites. Instead of

Overall James's conduct of government was clearly unsuccessful and he personally must take most of the blame . . . his extravagance and laziness were the major reasons for the decline in administrative efficiency which marked his reign.
—ALAN G. R. SMITH
historian, on James's
rule in England

The political lessons James had learned as king of Scotland did him little good in England, where the notion of representative government was much stronger. James brought to his new realm his belief in absolute, divine kingship, a position that immediately antagonized the members of Parliament.

instituting economies, however, James put on a dazzling month-long party for Anne's brother, Denmark's King Christian IV, who came over that summer for a visit. One drunken brawl went on for four days, and a witness described a masque in which an actress was so inebriated she fell on King Christian, who fell down himself when he tried to dance with her. James missed the irony of asking an increasingly Puritan Parliament to subsidize such behavior, even as he persecuted the Puritans.

In the aftermath of the Gunpowder Plot, James made a distinction between loyal Catholics and fa-

A delegation of Puritans appears before King James. James had alienated the Puritans, who wanted to reform the Anglican church, at the Hampton Court Conference in 1604. The king mistakenly saw the Puritans as English equivalents of the fanatic Kirkmen with whom he had struggled in Scotland.

Pope Paul V was greatly angered by James's abandonment of English Catholics and his attempts to put himself above papal authority. The pope tried to undermine the king by releasing letters that James sent many years earlier professing Catholic sentiments.

natics. Parliament drew up a new law that required all Englishmen to take an oath of allegiance affirming that the pope had no power to depose the king, foment rebellions, or encourage assassins. The combative Pope Paul V, however, rejected any infringement on his authority and forbade Catholics to take it. James responded with his "Apologie," a repetitive, impassioned defense of the oath. The Vatican counterattacked by releasing a letter James had sent to Rome many years before in which he had hinted at converting. The English were profoundly shocked. James had his Scottish secretary acknowledge authorship of the letter, but that did not explain how the king had come to sign it. James insisted he had never read this letter, but, in an astonishing feat of memory, he now remembered signing it accidentally, in a stack of other letters, many years earlier.

He reissued the "Apologie" with a long new preface, "A Premonition to All Christian Monarchies, Free Princes and States." The Premonition specifically warned James's fellow rulers how dangerous

Members of Parliament listen to the Speaker (seated, center) admonish a kneeling prisoner. James soon discovered that his financial position was dependent upon good relations with Parliament, which had to approve funds for the king. James deeply resented having to rely on Parliament and was generally uncooperative.

the papacy was both to their crowns and their lives. James's ambassadors presented elegant copies at all the European courts, where the documents were — to the king's unending amazement and chagrin —generally rejected or ignored.

James never liked persecuting Catholics, and Parliament's punitive acts of 1606 were so harsh as to be impractical. (How could a law banishing all Catholics from the court be enforced when the queen herself was a Catholic?) The king soon settled into a policy of lazy toleration.

If James was generally soft on Catholics, his contempt for his old enemies of the Scottish Kirk never abated. In August 1606 he summoned eight leading Kirkmen, including Andrew Melville, to a second conference at Hampton Court. The meeting was predictably contentious, and on November 30, Melville was summoned to answer charges that he had defamed Richard Bancroft, who had succeeded Whitgift as archbishop. James told the stubborn Kirkman to kneel before Bancroft. When he refused, attendants forced him down. He got away, however, and confronted the archbishop, charging him with corruption, superstition, and the persecution of the faithful. Melville was sent to the Tower and three years later banished to France. Besides robbing the Kirk of its independent leaders, James appointed a number of bishops and created a Scottish version of the High Commission, which had the power to fine and imprison nonconformists.

James's principle conflict during this time, however, was not religious but political. Without a strong, clever ruler, like Queen Elizabeth, who knew the art of dealing with Parliament, the Commons naturally developed its own leaders to assert its rights and increase its power. James could not hide his resentment at having to depend on a representative body, but "this eating canker of want," as he referred to his constant poverty, forced him to listen to Parliament's complaints. England was growing increasingly prosperous, but James was not: The sale of crown properties for short-term relief had reduced a fixed income already diminished by inflation. The extravagant spending of the king was never curbed, though Salisbury once made a striking effort to teach James the value of money. On receiving a check drawn by the king for 10,000 pounds as a gift for a royal favorite, Salisbury had the sum stacked in gold coins on a great table. James, astonished at the display, wanted to know whose money it was. It had been his, Salisbury told him, but he had given it away. James threw himself across the coins, pushed out a handful or two for the favorite, and asserted that he would keep the rest. Later, he resented how foolish Salisbury had made him look, and he did not learn the lesson. Because Salisbury could not get the king to economize, he had to find some way to pry subsidies from Parliament without surrendering the king's

> *Thus, I must say for Scotland . . . here I sit and govern it with my pen: I write and it is done: and by a clerk of the Council I govern Scotland now, which others could not do by sword.*
> —KING JAMES I
> to the English Parliament, 1607

James helped arrange the 1613 marriage of his first powerful court favorite, Robert Carr, to Frances Howard. James showered Carr with gifts and titles, making him earl of Somerset. Carr was the first Scot to sit in the House of Lords.

authority. To have Parliament vote a yearly royal allowance — after correcting the royal mistakes — would effectually end the tradition of government by king and council.

When Parliament convened in late 1606, James made his usual windy, vain, and petulant speech. He pressed for union with Scotland, but the Englishmen made many rude and inflammatory comments about their northern neighbor. Salisbury attempted to stave off a royal bankruptcy by selling crown lands and honors and by levying fees, or "impositions," on imports. He worried about the upcoming expiration of the king's subsidy, and he came up with a plan to resolve the question of finances permanently.

By 1610 Salisbury drew up a proposal, the Great Contract, in which the king agreed to surrender some of his ancient rights, including the hated right of purveyance, for a permanent annual parliamentary grant. The members were initially sympathetic despite being subjected to another of James's speeches on the divine right of kings. Parliament ended its first session with a tentative agreement, but during the break the members had time to reconsider their actions. When Parliament reconvened in November 1610, Salisbury was surprised to receive from the Commons a list of demands, including rigid enforcement of the laws against Catholics, reinstatement of nonconforming clergymen who had been dismissed from their places, an end to pluralism, reining in of the ecclesiastical courts, abolishment of impositions, and a substantial reduction of royal proclamations. James joked that he could unroll this long petition and use it as a tapestry.

Salisbury's Great Contract perished in the bitterness of the ensuing debates. Both sides were to blame for the failure of the contract: Parliament refused to address the very real issue of the need to increase royal revenues, and James, indignant at what he saw as Parliament's intrusion into royal prerogatives, became more autocratic in his treatment of the body. Each side soon hardened its position. James demanded more money. Parliament suggested sending all Scots home. One member pointedly brought up the precedent of King Richard II, who had been so stubbornly extravagant that a council had been set up to investigate his expenditures. The implication was clear: Richard had wasted his money on unpopular favorites, and his misdeeds had cost him both crown and life.

James dissolved the troublesome Parliament in February 1611, with no resolution of his fiscal crisis, and in the next 10 years he would only call Parliament once, for a turbulent 2-month session. Without a parliamentary subsidy the king was forced to squeeze every penny he could out of the various royal prerogatives that had already caused so many grievances. James, however, remained defiantly unconcerned. After dissolving Parliament he made a large bequest to a group of his favorites. In fact, he raised one of them, Robert Carr, to be Viscount Rochester, the first Scot to sit in the English House of Lords.

Robert Carr had by this time become very important to James. Queen Anne, who lost a baby in 1606 and another in 1607, had turned away from James and occupied herself with her clothes, masques, and jewels. Prince Henry had grown up to be a popular, handsome youth who spent many hours every day training and exercising, but he was too devout, upright, and conservative ever to be close to his father. James turned increasingly for friendship and affection to his favorites.

Carr had been a page at James's court in Scotland. After some years in France, he was invited to the court in England. He was a tall, red-haired, blue-eyed man with a winning smile and no other accomplishments in particular. The 41-year-old love-starved monarch soon raised the 19-year-old favorite to be a gentleman of the bedchamber, leaning on him in public, pinching his cheek, smoothing his clothes, and showering him with favors. James taught him Latin and made him a knight, and when the young man needed some property, James dispossessed Sir Walter Raleigh's family and gave him

RICHARD II

As James became more autocratic in his dealings with Parliament, many representatives began to compare him pointedly to Richard II. The 14th-century English king had been forced to abdicate because of his inability to placate Parliament.

75

their house, which caused a wave of public sympathy for Raleigh and increased the king's unpopularity.

In what would ultimately lead to the worst scandal of his reign, James helped Carr get a wife. When James first came to England, he had demonstrated his gratitude to the Essex and Howard families for their support by impulsively sponsoring a marriage between the 14-year-old son of the earl of Essex, and Frances Howard, the striking, willful 13-year-old daughter of Thomas Howard, earl of Suffolk, and niece of Henry Howard, earl of Northampton. After the wedding, the groom had been sent to France to be educated, while the bride remained to grace the Stuart court. By the time Essex returned, in 1609, his lady had moved from an affair with Prince Henry to a more serious liaison with Carr. Lady Essex would have nothing to do with her husband, and her family tried to get her marriage annulled.

James set up a commission to secure the annulment. When the commission balked, he added two more officials with the "correct" point of view. Meanwhile, Carr's good friend Sir Thomas Overbury, afraid of having to compete with the new bride for the royal favorite's attention, objected so vehemently to the marriage that Carr contrived to get him out of the way. Overbury was hustled off to the Tower, where he died suddenly on September 15, 1613. Ten days later, the king's commission granted the annulment, and on December 26, the court celebrated the wedding. James gave the newlyweds 10,000 pounds he could ill afford and made Carr earl of Somerset. At the time, James had no suspicion of the trouble the Somersets would cause him.

On the foreign front during this first decade of James's reign in England, the king initiated a destructive policy in Ireland that continues to have consequences today. The armies of Elizabeth had put down a major rebellion in time for James to receive the submissions of the Irish leaders Hugh O'Neill, the earl of Tyrone, and Rory McDonnell, the earl of Tyrconnell. The powers of these great chief-

Hugh O'Neill, earl of Tyrone, was an Irish chieftain who had led an unsuccessful revolt against the English under Elizabeth. When O'Neill fled Ireland in 1607, James confiscated his Ulster lands for English and Scottish settlers, thus planting the seeds of the Protestant-Catholic conflict in Ireland.

tains diminished as the English influence increased, and in September 1607, fearing for their lives and hoping to find support abroad, the earls fled Ulster, the great northern province of Ireland. James gave their lands — and all the lands that fell to the Crown — to Scottish and English settlers, reducing the native Irish to a position of great inferiority in terms of property and power. The new settlers were, of course, Protestant. The vast majority of the country, however, was staunchly Catholic. Thus began the religious and political divisions that have since haunted Ireland.

One of the most important foreign policy decisions of these years was the pledge of support Salisbury drew out of James in 1608 for the Dutch, who were negotiating their Twelve Years' Truce with a weakened and humiliated Spain. Against his own inclinations, James promised to back the Dutch if Spain broke the treaty. His decision established England as the champion of Protestant Europe.

On the domestic front, the sad episode of Lady Arabella Stuart's marriage occurred in 1610. James's English cousin had kept herself honorably clear of all conspiracies and scandals. She fell in love, however, with William Seymour, a quiet and bookish young man who had his own dynastic claim to the English throne. A child born of their union might pose a serious threat to the Stuart succession, so James forbade the marriage. When he heard that they had married secretly, he had them arrested. Seymour escaped, but Arabella was sent to the Tower, where she spent four years before she went insane and died.

In May 1612 Salisbury died. James, who never lost his morbid fear of death, reacted indifferently, as he had done at the death of Maitland, and he vowed not to give any other man the power Cecil had enjoyed. He passed responsibility for the treasury to a commission headed by the greedy Northampton and increasingly turned for assistance to Somerset and the other "creatures," as he tenderly called his favorites. This growing reliance on court favorites widened the divisions between the king and the English people, and in an additional antagonistic move, in October 1612 James had his

Lady Arabella Stuart, in disguise, attempts to flee England in 1610. James forbade his cousin to marry a man who would have strengthened her claim to the crown, but Arabella wed him secretly and tried to escape to France. She was captured and imprisoned in the Tower of London, where she died in 1615.

James's eldest son, Henry, prince of Wales, died on May 24, 1612. Unlike the timid king, Henry had been a strong athlete and soldier. The death of the popular prince was a blow to many who thought he would make a better king than his father.

mother's body brought to Westminster Abbey, where it was laid to rest in a larger and richer tomb than that of England's Queen Elizabeth, which was nearby.

In November the king suffered a great loss when the heir to the throne, Prince Henry, fell sick and died quickly of typhoid fever. They had not been close — the prince was no friend of the slippery favorites who flocked about the throne. Nevertheless, the king's grief was so great it made him ill.

Soon, however, the king had other matters to occupy him. Before his death, Salisbury had found a match for Princess Elizabeth that would help hold together the Protestant Union, a coalition of European states that had formed an alliance against the

The ships of Frederick V, elector of the Palatinate, arrive in England in October 1612. Frederick was married to James's daughter Elizabeth in February 1613, much to the delight of the English, who firmly supported an alliance with the Protestant German state.

Catholic continental powers. The bland, handsome bridegroom, Frederick V, elector of the Palatinate (a territory in central Germany) and a militant Calvinist, was already in England when Prince Henry died. The elaborate, expensive wedding was celebrated on Valentine's Day, 1613, and James wept to see the happy pair sail away on April 25. Frederick and Elizabeth would soon become embroiled in the Protestant struggle in central Europe, and James would never see his daughter again.

By the end of the year, James's financial situation had become so desperate that he was forced to summon another Parliament. He said he hoped this would be a "Parliament of love." He pointed out how great his expenses were, particularly for his son's funeral and his daughter's wedding, and he hoped the assembly would grant him sufficient allowance. He also suggested that Parliament should only consider bills proposed by him. However, James did not offer to make any significant concessions or even to promise any economies. The 1614 "Addled Parliament" (so called because it did not pass a single act) erupted in bitter debates, and the king left an account of his frustrations in a letter. "The House of Commons," he wrote, "is a body without a head. The members give their opinions in a disorderly manner. At their meetings nothing is heard but cries, shouts and confusion. I am surprised that my ancestors should ever have permitted such an institution to come into existence."

Strangely enough, James's criticism of Parliament was written not to an Englishman, but to Don Diego de Sarmiento, the Spanish ambassador. Sarmiento had arrived in London in May 1613 to help swing James from the Protestant powers. He was a warm, bold, brilliant man and had become the king's close friend. To the distress of his council, James seemed to think of the foreign ambassador as his own adviser; he consulted with him frequently on matters of state. Sarmiento's advice agreed with what James was hearing from the pro-Spanish Northampton and Somerset; he dissolved the Addled Parliament in June 1614, not two months after it had opened, and sent four of its most troublesome members to the Tower. They were soon released, but the hostility James had aroused did not disappear. In his dealings with Parliament, James was alternately weak and tyrannical, arrogant and familiar, condescending and rude. Although the king now held power, the "body without a head" was growing stronger. It would not be forever patient with the autocratic Stuart manner.

George Villiers
Duke of Buckingham

7

The Rising Star

James's most pressing problem was to support his establishment without any parliamentary funding. To that end, the king decided to negotiate a match between his heir — the melancholy, bookish Prince Charles — and the Spanish *infanta* (royal princess) Maria Anna. James was convinced that he would receive from the Spanish a dowry large enough to pay all his debts, and he set his ministers to work on the negotiations. Northampton had died a week after Parliament was dissolved; Suffolk was now lord treasurer, and Somerset, the new lord chamberlain, started a sort of national fund-raising appeal.

Though Somerset still exerted himself on the king's behalf, it became clear that he had changed. James had declared that he loved Somerset "above all men living," but great power had made the favorite haughty. He had become rude to everyone — even, occasionally, to James. There was no public breach between the two, but a widening distance that grieved the king. Without really intending to replace Somerset, James turned his attention to someone else.

George Villiers was tall, graceful, athletic, and attractive. He caught the king's eye sometime in August 1614. The 28 year old had, in fact, been

> *Buckingham's attraction was obviously strongly physical: with his dark eyes and chestnut hair he intoxicated the King. . . . In short, Buckingham was dashing.*
> —ANTONIA FRASER
> English biographer, on James's final favorite

The handsome George Villiers was the final and most powerful of James's court favorites. The youngest son of an impoverished family, he rose from his initial position as royal cupbearer to become duke of Buckingham in 1623.

introduced into the court by Lord Chancellor Elles-mere, George Abbott, the archbishop of Canterbury, and Secretary Sir Ralph Winwood, all of whom opposed Somerset and the Howard family. Two months later, Villiers was a royal cupbearer (Somerset blocked his appointment as gentleman of the bedchamber), and a circle of ambitious courtiers began to form around him. Villiers's appeal for James seems to have been largely paternal. He called James his "dear Dad," and James, in turn, called Villiers by the Scottish endearment "Steenie," ostensibly for Villiers's resemblance to a portrait of St. Stephen, the first Christian martyr. James defined their close relationship to his startled council: "Christ had his John, and I have my George."

In April 1615 Villiers was knighted and made a gentleman of the bedchamber. Somerset, unable to check Villiers's rise, began to worry about losing his influence. He knew that as soon as he fell from favor, the enemies he had made at court would clamor for his head. In July Somerset went to James and demanded a general pardon for any offenses he might have committed in the years of his service to the king. Although James agreed to the pardon, the lord chancellor would not seal it. James abandoned the matter and went hunting. The pardon was never sealed.

Soon the full lurid story of the Essex divorce scandal and the even more shocking subsequent events, successfully hidden for two years, burst into public view. The revelation began when an apothecary's boy, convinced he was dying, confessed to the murder of a Tower prisoner. The boy told the English envoy in Brussels that on September 15, 1613, he had administered an enema to Sir Thomas Overbury, the man who had tried so hard to prevent Somerset's marriage. Overbury had not been well since his imprisonment, and an enema was a common treatment for general ailments. However, this enema was filled with mercury, and Overbury suffered a horrible death from poisoning.

The envoy passed the story on to Secretary Winwood, who searched quietly until he had enough corroborating evidence to place the matter before

The poet and scholar Sir Thomas Overbury was the victim of court intrigue when he violently opposed Somerset's marriage to Frances Howard. James had him imprisoned in the Tower, where he was slowly poisoned to death on the orders of the new countess of Somerset.

the king. James, profoundly shaken, gave Winwood permission for a thorough investigation, and the secretary ferreted out the details. Lady Essex had placed her own man, Richard Weston, as Overbury's jailer. A false apothecary named Franklin had procured arsenic, and a court madame named Mrs. Turner had arranged for dishes laced with the deadly element to be carried to the Tower. The conspirators had poisoned the poor man all summer, but they only made him sick. They were thwarted, for a while, by the lieutenant of the Tower, Sir Gervase Helwys, who had discovered the plot but was afraid to expose it because he assumed the powerful favorite was behind it.

In September 1615 a full written report was passed on to Sir Edward Coke, chief justice of the King's Bench, and he began an investigation. Although no hard evidence of Somerset's guilt was ever found, his behavior at this time, as he raced around collecting and altering or destroying old letters, was most suspicious. He begged the king to protect him, but James, afraid for his own reputation and disgusted by the matter, told him he could do nothing for him.

Somerset and his countess were arrested in October 1615. Weston, Franklin, Mrs. Turner, and Lieutenant Helwys were all tried and hanged by Christmas. The countess of Somerset went on trial on May 24, 1616, before the attorney general, Sir Francis Bacon. She pleaded guilty and begged for mercy. Somerset at first had been frantic, going so far as to threaten James with hints about damaging secrets he might reveal in court. James took the precaution of stationing men with large cloaks near Somerset throughout his 12-hour trial, with orders to muffle him if necessary. But once in court, the earl maintained his innocence with dignity. He was found guilty nonetheless.

Despite their convictions, the guilty pair escaped the executioner. James commuted their death sentences, and the couple stayed in the Tower until 1622, when they were allowed to go live in an insignificant country manor. The king stipulated that they had to stay together and could go no more than

Sir Edward Coke, lord chief justice of James's court, conducted the investigation into the murder of Overbury. Both the earl and countess of Somerset were found guilty, but James commuted their death sentences to six years' imprisonment in the Tower followed by exile from the royal court.

three miles from their house. The rumor spread at court that the Somersets were no longer speaking, which amused the king. Although James easily survived the fall of Somerset, the reputation of his government did not. The doings at his court, always salacious, had now been shown to be sordid, and James never regained the respect or the affection of his people.

The declining years of James's reign featured the

Sir Edward Coke published works on English common law in which he argued that the judiciary stood above the king in matters of justice. Offended by Coke's independence, James dismissed him from his post as chief justice in 1616.

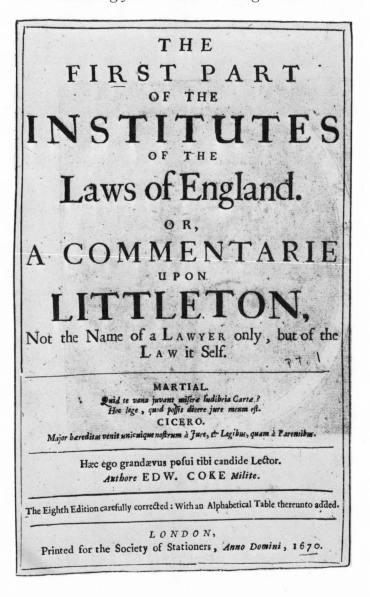

ascendancy of his beloved Steenie, "the handsomest bodied man in England," who was made duke of Buckingham in 1623 and became finally a sort of surrogate king, distributing favors and offices, and even formulating policies, sometimes against the inclinations of the melancholy, weeping, increasingly feeble monarch. Buckingham was a more confident, polished, and agreeable gentleman than Somerset, but he was not without his detractors. Queen Anne did not like him at first, so he set himself to win her over. The crown prince — "Baby Charles," as James called him — had several sharp public conflicts with the favorite. Whether from natural inclination or the shrewdest self-interest, Buckingham decided to make friends with the priggish, colorless boy. In June 1618 Buckingham presented "the Prince's Feast," a sumptuous banquet in Charles's honor. Charles, always in awe of his learned father, was glad to make peace with the glamorous Buckingham.

As Buckingham's power and influence grew, the decline of the Howards was assured. The family, the center of the pro-Spanish faction at court, still held considerable power and tried to keep it by bringing to court a succession of eligible young men in the hope of replacing Buckingham. The king saw through their clumsy plot and sent the young hopefuls from the court.

Buckingham counterattacked with greater skill and success. An investigation at the treasury exposed a system of regular bribes taken by Suffolk's obnoxious wife on every official transaction. James ordered her out of town, and Suffolk lost his post. Buckingham replaced him as treasurer with a self-made city merchant, Lionel Cranfield, who would prove to be an excellent bureaucrat. The threat of an investigation into the admiralty accounts brought the resignation of another important Howard — the old, nearly senile earl of Nottingham. So many Howards went to the Tower that one wit joked they could form their own privy council there. Buckingham quietly replaced them with middle-class civil servants, men he could easily control.

Buckingham also engineered the fall of Chief Jus-

> *Skillfully he [Buckingham] pretended to return James's love. The King tells him to make his letters merry and he replies: 'How can I but write merrily when he is so I love best and beyond all the world.'*
> —D. HARRIS WILLSON
> historian

James and his heir, Prince Charles, attend a banquet with a group of Spanish ambassadors. James and his son negotiated with Spain for six fruitless years to arrange a marriage between Charles and the Spanish infanta Maria.

tice Coke. Coke had angered the king in 1606, when he told James that though the king was above all men, he must still be under God and the law. He was a staunch defender of English common-law rights, which James never comprehended, and championed an independent judiciary. In June 1616, after a quarrel concerning the king's authority over judges, James suspended Coke.

At the same time, Buckingham's large family, seeking advancement, descended on the court. His greedy, meddling mother, Lady Compton, selected Coke's lovely daughter Frances as a suitable mate for her unremarkable son John. When Coke was told that compliance could restore his fortunes, he responded rudely that the price of the king's favor was too high, and his suspension became a dismissal. Some months out of power changed his mind, however, and in September 1617 Sir John Villiers married Frances Coke. Coke was restored to the privy council, but not to his post as chief justice.

If Buckingham was James's great joy, money — or the lack of it — remained his great sorrow. Cranfield managed to pinch an income together through reforms and economies, but the careless king's "necessities" continued to outstrip his budget. Poverty influenced every aspect of the king's domestic and foreign policy, including his long preoccupation with arranging a Spanish marriage for Baby Charles in order to get the large Spanish dowry. Sarmiento, now Count Gondomar, also supported the marriage, believing that such a match would lead to the restoration of Catholicism first in England, then in all of Europe. However, Gondomar grossly underestimated the strength of English Protestants, who hated and feared the idea of any sort of Spanish-Catholic alliance.

In May 1615 Gondomar gave James a list of the points Spain required as a basis for any marriage negotiations: the relaxation of England's anti-Catholic laws; a dispensation from the pope; a promise that children of the marriage be raised as Catholics and not barred from the English succession on religious grounds; and an open Catholic household in England for the infanta, with a chapel, a burial ground, even a Catholic wet nurse for the babies. Knowing that Parliament would never agree to such demands, James misled his council as to the terms and sent an ambassador to Spain to conclude a treaty.

But the process was slow and the king's need pressing. In April 1616 James sold the "Cautionary Towns" — Flushing, Brill, and Rammekens, held since the reign of Elizabeth as pledges for large English loans — back to the Dutch, cancelling loans worth three times as much as the sum he accepted. The king also got some shameful income by retailing baronetcies, knighthoods, and even peerages. Then a scheme that offered the possibility of fabulous wealth captured his fancy.

Sir Walter Raleigh, who still languished in the Tower, made a last attempt to secure his release. The great Elizabethan adventurer, who had been to the New World in 1591 and sailed 120 miles up the Orinoco River in Guiana, had heard stories of a golden land there called El Dorado. Desperate now to get out of prison, he offered to sail back to claim the gold for James.

Gondomar was outraged. As Raleigh very well knew, there was a Spanish settlement, San Thomé, on the Orinoco. Raleigh could hardly take gold from that vicinity without a fight, but James made Raleigh promise not to harm any Spaniards. Furthermore, the king assured Gondomar that if Raleigh broke that promise, he would send him bound to

The famed Elizabethan soldier, explorer, and scholar Sir Walter Raleigh spent most of James's reign imprisoned in the Tower on treason charges. James released him to make a gold-prospecting expedition to Guiana in 1617, but the mission failed, and Raleigh was executed after his return to England.

This fanciful portrait shows the entire Stuart family. To the left of James (seated) are Princes Charles and Henry and Queen Anne; Elizabeth and Frederick stand to the right with their children. Two daughters of James and Anne who died young are seated below the king.

Spain for punishment. Raleigh, leading a squadron of 14 ships on this impossible mission, sailed from Plymouth, England, in the summer of 1617.

At about the same time, James went on a visit to Scotland that nearly bankrupted both his kingdoms. James had not seen his native land for 14 years and insisted on the progress, despite united opposition from his councilors. He was exuberantly welcomed all along the way, except by his old foes in the Kirk. When he attempted to establish Anglican control over the Scottish Protestants, both the Kirk and the Lords of the Congregation, who dominated the Scottish parliament, opposed him with their usual energy. In 1618 a General Assembly at Perth, shamelessly packed with James's bishops and newly made peers, accepted the Anglican ceremonies imposed on the Scottish church, but those churches that actually instituted the changes lost their congregations. The Scots fiercely resisted any meddling in their religious affairs, and the enmity between Anglicans and Presbyterians grew.

James had begun his trip to Scotland full of hope and youthful vigor, but he came back in September 1618 feeling old again, miserable with gout and arthritis, and more tormented by his straitened circumstances than ever. Greater disappointments greeted him in England. First he learned that King Philip had raised his demands. England's anti-Catholic laws would have to be repealed before the infanta could leave Spain and before any part of her dowry could be paid. The Anglican theologians were not to attempt to convert the infanta, and her proposed chapel at the English court was to be open to the English public. James knew that Parliament would never agree to such demands.

More bad news arrived when the first survivors of Raleigh's expedition returned. The little fleet had faced contrary winds, a hurricane, the equatorial doldrums, and an epidemic of fever before reaching Guiana. Sick with fever himself, Raleigh sent his faithful lieutenant, Lawrence Keymis, up the Orinoco. There had never been much hope of avoiding conflict with the Spaniards at San Thomé, and when the Spanish fired, the English responded. Keymis and his men took the town, but the Spaniards hid in the jungle and picked off the victors, who could hardly go out looking for food, much less mines of gold. After a wretched month at San Thomé, Keymis returned to the ships, gave Raleigh the bad news, and then killed himself. Raleigh's men threatened a mutiny, so he was forced to return to England. When he sailed into Portsmouth in June 1618, he was quickly arrested.

Gondomar insisted that James fulfill his pledge by sending Raleigh to Spain for punishment, and to the horror of the English, James agreed. Only the better judgment of the Spanish king prevented this outrage. Instead, to placate Gondomar, James freed all the Catholic priests in English prisons. The king appointed a commission to dispose of the anachronistic hero. The commission decided that no trial was needed, because Raleigh was still under a death sentence from 1603. Despite great public sympathy for Raleigh, the king sent him to the scaffold. Running his finger along the executioner's ax, Raleigh said, "Sharp medicine, but a sure cure for all diseases." When a bystander directed him to face east, the Elizabethan hero said, "What matter how the head be, so the heart be right?" For many Englishmen, the heart in England was no longer right.

8

The Bitter Seeds

James spent most of his reign preoccupied with domestic issues. The one great foreign policy crisis he encountered found him sadly wanting, and he had no skillful councilors to advise him on such matters.

In 1617 the aged and childless Holy Roman Emperor Matthias attempted to guarantee that his family, the powerful Austrian Catholic Habsburgs, would retain control of the eastern portion of the empire by raising his cousin Ferdinand of Styria to be king of Bohemia (modern western Czechoslovakia). The Protestant nobles of Bohemia, however, were violently opposed to Austrian and Catholic rule. In May 1618 they captured the emperor's representatives at the palace in Prague, the Bohemian capital, and hurled them out a window. The "Defenestration of Prague" began the brutal central European conflict between Catholics and Protestants that is known as the Thirty Years' War.

Most of Bohemia went over to the rebels, who asked James, as a great Protestant leader, for help. Spain was tied by blood and treaty to Austria, but the Spanish treasury was low and the truce with the Dutch would soon expire, raising Spanish fears of a renewed Spanish-Dutch conflict. Gondomar conceived a clever strategy to keep England neutral:

It seems to me that the intelligence of this King has diminished. . . . His mind uses its powers only for a short time, but in the long run he is cowardly. His timidity increases day by day as old age carries him into apprehensions and vices diminish his intelligence.
—COUNT LEVENEUR DE TILLIÈRES French ambassador, on James's decline in old age

In November 1619 Elector Frederick was crowned king of Bohemia. His reign lasted only until the following November, when he and Elizabeth were forced to flee Prague by an invading Catholic army. The crisis in central Europe would be a foreign policy disaster for James.

King Philip asked James to mediate a peace. The plan appealed both to James's vanity and to his desire to stave off a costly European war. He sent a ridiculously ostentatious mission off to mediate, but neither the Habsburgs nor the Bohemians were interested in mediation. The embassy trotted around Europe trying to drum up support for James's peace initiative, spending money James could not spare and making him a laughingstock.

In March 1619 Matthias died; five months later Ferdinand was elected emperor. The Bohemians immediately rejected Ferdinand, formally deposed him as king of Bohemia, and offered their crown to an impetuous and fiery young Protestant leader: Frederick V, James's son-in-law. Frederick sent to James for advice, but when he received no reply he accepted. In November 1619 Frederick and Elizabeth were crowned king and queen of Bohemia.

James was in a dilemma. He was pleased to see his son-in-law and daughter win crowns, but if he gave them any support, he would lose Spain and the infanta's dowry. Besides, Frederick was a usurper crowned by rebels who had deposed their rightful king, an unpardonable crime to the author of *Trew Law* and *Basilikon Doron*. The matter was further complicated by the enormous sympathy in England for Frederick and Elizabeth. The English people favored sending help, but James characteristically dawdled. He wasted time puzzling over the Bohemian constitution and exploring the legitimacy of Frederick's title. Meanwhile, Maximilian of Bavaria offered to fight for Ferdinand if the emperor would reward him with Frederick's state, the Palatinate.

Gondomar quickly discovered that James had no intention of going to war and informed Philip that Spain and Austria were free to move against the Bohemians. In August 1620 a Bavarian army under the brilliant Flemish general John Tserclaes, count of Tilly, moved against Prague, while a Spanish army invaded the Lower Palatinate. In November Tilly's forces routed the Bohemians at the Battle of White Mountain, west of Prague, and Frederick and

King James would almost certainly have advised Frederick to refuse the Bohemian offer. . . . For Frederick to accept the crown belonging to Ferdinand meant conniving with rebels.

—G. P. V. AKRIGG
Canadian historian, on the crisis that launched the Thirty Years' War

Elizabeth fled. "The Winter King" had not quite held his crown a full year, but his Bohemian dream was over, and his legitimate rule in the Palatinate was now in jeopardy.

James wept pitifully when he heard the news and told Gondomar that he would have to defend his "children." The king promised to defend the Palatinate, which caused great rejoicing, but necessitated the raising of an army. James realized his next bitter step was to convene Parliament, the only source of funding for such an enterprise. The king balked and began to reconsider when Gondomar told him that Spain's invasion of the Palatinate was the surest way to peace: If Frederick would renounce his claim to Bohemia, he could have the Palatinate back.

Parliament met late in January 1621. James asked for 500,000 pounds, an absurdly low figure to support the 30,000-man army he envisaged. Parliament voted only 160,000 pounds for the king's other necessities. The members wanted a detailed plan for the defense of the Palatinate before they voted money for it. James was delighted to get some cash, however, and no doubt quickly gave some of

On May 23, 1618, a group of Protestant Bohemian nobles at the palace in Prague hurled two imperial commissioners and a secretary from Catholic Austria out a window. This event, known to history as the Defenestration of Prague, sparked the Thirty Years' War in Europe.

it, as Parliament had feared, to Inigo Jones, who was building him a spectacular banqueting house at Whitehall, the perfect spot for an Anglo-Spanish wedding. Although delay would be fatal for Frederick, James let the Palatinate slide, and Parliament turned with a vengeance to its grievances.

The first was the abuse of monopolies, the exclusive rights granted by the Crown to control particular commodities or services with the resulting power to fix prices and eliminate competition. They were, in essence, licenses to get rich. Although the granting of monopolies was strictly regulated by law, in practice they were common, deeply resented burdens that enriched court favorites while raising prices and lowering the quality of goods. The Buckingham family was profiting enormously from them, and when the Commons began vigorously debating this issue, Buckingham saw that the members were aiming at him. Sir Edward Coke, a leader in this turbulent Parliament, called the favorite "the grievance of grievances." Buckingham begged James to

In 1621 Sir Francis Bacon, then high lord chancellor, was tried by Parliament for accepting bribes in court. When the statesman, scientist, and scholar was fined and dismissed from his post, he warned James that Parliament was assuming too much authority.

dissolve Parliament, but the king could not do so without a Palatinate solution. With no alternative, Buckingham abandoned his relatives and appeared before the Commons to denounce the abuse of monopolies.

The Commons uncovered considerable corruption in the courts, where crown referees had allowed so many irregular monopolies. In particular, they gathered sufficient evidence to impeach Coke's old enemy, Sir Francis Bacon, now viscount St. Albans and lord high chancellor of England, on bribery charges. Bacon tried to resist, warning James that "those who strike at your Chancellor, it is much to be feared, will strike at your Crown," but James let him go. The chancellor resigned his office in April 1621.

While Frederick's situation worsened, James tried to avoid a commitment. In October, news reached England that the Protestant Union was tottering. The Palatinate was almost entirely in the hands of Maximilian and the Bavarians. Parliament reconvened, but the king, weary of the long crisis, had retired to the country. The Commons drafted a "Petition" to the king, asking that all the anti-Catholic laws be strictly enforced, war be declared on Spain, and Prince Charles marry a Protestant.

"God give me patience!" James exclaimed when he heard of it. Gondomar insolently lectured him that unless he "punished" Parliament, he "would have ceased to be a king here." James sent a strong letter chastising and threatening Parliament, whereupon the members drew up a second "Petition" that referred solemnly to "the ancient liberty of Parliament for freedom of speech, jurisdiction, and just censure." James responded hotly, blaming Frederick for the war, praising the king of Spain, and informing the Commons that their vaunted privileges were derived entirely "from the grace and permission" of the king. In December 1621 the Commons drew up a grave and eloquent "Protestation," which claimed freedom of debate and freedom from arrest as "the ancient and undoubted birthright and inheritance" of all Englishmen.

Gondomar frankly doubted that the great king of Spain could go on negotiating with any monarch who permitted his subjects to be so rebellious, and Buckingham and Prince Charles shared his sentiments. On December 30 James made a show of tearing up the offensive "Protestation" and dissolved Parliament, a step all his other councilors had desperately opposed. Parliament had made no provision for the Palatinate. Frederick's capital, Heidelberg, fell in September 1622, and he soon became an elector without an electorate. James tried to raise money for Frederick with new impositions and a benevolence — a forced loan — but he could hardly wage war without Parliament.

Queen Anne, from whom James had long been

Queen Anne died in March 1619. The treasury was nearly broke because of James's extravagance and his recent official state visit to Scotland, and Anne's body had to be kept unburied for nearly three months until funds could be provided for her funeral.

separated, but with whom he had always been on good terms, died in March 1619. The king, feeling increasingly isolated, turned more and more to Steenie and Baby Charles. The companionable trio was enlarged in 1620 when Buckingham married an heiress, Lady Katherine Manners. James eagerly adopted her as "Baby Kate" and took enormous pleasure in all the details of her domesticity, especially in her babies. Buckingham and his family clearly provided the aging king with the only real sense of family he had ever had.

James was so crippled with gout and arthritis, so enfeebled by his gorging on fresh fruits and overindulgence in sweet wines, that he could hardly walk and frequently had to be carried. Notoriously careless about his health, he was subject to chronic colds. He had suffered great agonies with kidney stones just after the queen's death and was terrified of a recurrence. He was increasingly careless in his personal habits, dirty, fearful, and subject to long fits of weeping.

His foreign policy reverted to the fantasy of a Spanish alliance. With some difficulty, he extracted a promise from Frederick to renounce Bohemia and beg forgiveness of the emperor. Then James heard that Ferdinand planned to declare Maximilian of Bavaria the new elector of the Palatinate he had conquered. James raged and waited for Spain either to persuade Austria to withdraw its forces or join England in an attack to drive them out.

So much now depended on the Spanish marriage — peace in Germany, the restoration of Frederick in the Palatinate, the dowry — that James was stupefied when he learned in August 1622 that the impossible Spanish demands had been raised again at the bidding of a papal commission. English laws against Catholics would have to be repealed and their freedom of worship allowed. The infanta's church had to be open to the public and her priests exempt from English law. She was to control her children's education until the girls were 12 and the boys reached 14.

James sent an ambassador, Endymion Porter, to

> *Not only was he ageing, sick and unhappy, but he was confronted increasingly with the shrewish coalition of Prince Charles and Buckingham.*
> —ANTONIA FRASER
> English biographer, on the bullying of the elderly James by his son and favorite

99

Spain with a letter from the privy council formally requesting Spanish assistance in the Palatinate, with a firm threat to end the long marriage negotiations. Porter came home in January 1623 with some relaxed terms from Spain. In return for a 500,000-pound dowry, there should be tolerance for English Catholics. Some mutually agreeable settlement would be worked out for the Palatinate. James and Charles eagerly signed these vague accords. Carried away by the excitement, Steenie and Baby Charles came up with a plan to get the Spanish infanta. James agreed to it, even though he could see what a rash and foolish idea it was.

On February 18, 1623, traveling under the false names Tom and Jack Smith and sporting fake beards, Steenie and Charles crossed the Thames on the first leg of their "secret" mission to Spain. In Paris they observed the 14-year-old princess, Henrietta Maria, but did not stop long. They rode into Madrid on March 7, to the inestimable delight of Gondomar, who thought Prince Charles's conversion must be imminent. The king of Spain was less enthusiastic. Philip III had died in March 1621 and

En route to Spain to negotiate for a bride, Prince Charles saw Henrietta Maria, sister to Louis XIII, in Paris. He remembered the pretty French princess after the Spanish match fell through, and the two were married by proxy in May 1625.

his son, who inherited the crown as Philip IV, had made him a deathbed promise not to marry the infanta to Charles. The princess herself had expressed her desire to enter a convent rather than marry a heretic.

Charles and Buckingham threw off their disguises, sent to James for money, clothes, servants, even "tilting [jousting] equipment," and began the negotiations. James also sent Church of England chaplains and paraphernalia, all of which were indignantly rejected by the Spanish. James tried to put on a brave face and sent cheery letters, full of chat. "I wear Steenie's picture in a blue ribbon under my washcoat next my heart," he wrote, and, to Charles, "My sweet Baby, for God's sake, and your dad's, put not yourself in hazard by any violent exercise long as ye are there."

Charles had now decided he was in love. "Babie Charles himself is so touched at the heart," Steenie wrote dad, "that he confesses all he ever yet saw is nothing to her." But the prince was never able to see the lady alone. He spent a lot of time staring at her at the theater, and when he did get to meet with her, both his clothes and his conversation were strictly prescribed by the highly formal Spanish court.

There were some positive developments. King Philip ordered the release of all English galley slaves, the great playwright Lope de Vega wrote a piece in Charles's honor, and the renowned artist Velázquez painted his portrait, but the marriage talks stalled. The Spanish were waiting for a dispensation from Pope Gregory XV. Philip had secretly urged the pope not to grant it, but the pope felt that an Anglo-Spanish match might ease the situation of the English Catholics. He sent the dispensation but added new conditions that made the marriage impossible: English Catholics had to be permitted to take an oath submitted by the pope instead of the oath of allegiance, James had to get his council and Parliament to agree to the demand, and Philip had to swear to enforce the treaty's terms.

Buckingham, who saw that the marriage negotiations were over, behaved rudely to his hosts, but

James reads a set of demands from Spain regarding the marriage of Charles to the infanta, while a scowling Spanish ambassador looks on. James knew Parliament would never agree to the demands, but fearing that the Spanish would hold Charles and Buckingham prisoners, he signed the agreement.

the lovelorn Charles amazed everyone by blithely agreeing to everything the pope had asked. He declared that James would suspend the anti-Catholic laws and press Parliament for its consent, the laws would definitely be repealed within three years, and Charles would even let the infanta's priests try to convert him without ever saying a word against her Catholic faith. The prince probably expected to ignore such promises when he got his bride to England.

Suspicious of Charles's wholehearted agreement, Philip increased the demands. James had to proclaim the suspension of the anti-Catholic laws, swear never to reimpose them, and secure the concurrence of Parliament. Worst of all, the infanta was to remain in Spain one full year after the marriage to make sure the English kept their promises. Buckingham was furious; Charles, wounded and withdrawn. They sent the new demands to James.

After a month in which he had heard no word from his sweet boys, the king got this message. The news had "stricken him dead," he wrote. His worst fear — that they were prisoners — seemed about to come true. "Alas, I now repent me sore that ever I suffered you to go away," he wrote in desperation. In his terror, he agreed to everything and urged Charles to sign whatever was put before him, marry, and come home. If the infanta did not follow, the Anglican church could annul the marriage.

The marriage articles were ratified by the weeping king and his council at Whitehall on July 20. On July 25, Charles signed a treaty in Madrid. He accepted all the Spanish demands, though there was no definite agreement about the dowry, the Palatinate, or even the date of the wedding. He left a signed proxy for the marriage with his ambassador, but he also left secret orders not to produce the proxy with-

Great Britain's war council meets to discuss the conflict with Spain. In 1623 Charles and Buckingham returned to England determined to declare war on Spain. James, virtually insensible to matters of foreign policy, continued to push Parliament for a treaty with Spain.

out further instructions. Their adventure a fiasco, Baby Charles and Steenie sailed home. They landed at Portsmouth on October 5, and England was so delighted to get them back safe, still Protestant, and with the prince as yet unmarried, that they were greeted with tumultuous rejoicing. Their "old dad" laughed and cried as he embraced his boys.

Charles and Buckingham brought back with them a passionate hatred of the Spanish. "I am ready to conquer Spain," Charles informed his father, "if you will allow me to do it." Carried along on a wave of popularity, the prince and the favorite combined to rush and bully the poor old king into summoning Parliament in 1624. James made a meandering speech, apologizing for his policies and asking for advice on the Spanish treaties. Taking him at his word, Parliament advised him to reject the treaty and go to war. James sent a furious reply, but Buckingham and the prince interpreted his words to mean the opposite of what he had said. Raging and weeping, the king left London.

James seemed to realize he had lost control to his boys but did not move to regain it. Still, there were moments when he reasserted himself. When Buckingham vengefully moved to impeach Treasurer Cranfield, mostly for having supported James's peace policy, the king warned him that in using the dangerous machinery of impeachment he would be "making a rod with which you will be scourged yourself." With eerie prescience he chastised Charles for "weakening the crown," exclaiming that the prince "would live to have his bellyful of Parliaments."

Meanwhile, Buckingham and Charles pursued another marriage alliance, still Catholic but this time anti-Spanish, with Henrietta Maria, the pretty young princess they had seen in Paris. Though James had promised Parliament no marriage treaty would ever again include concessions to English Catholics, France naturally expected the same offers that had been made to Spain, and James could not say no to his boys. In November 1624 James ignored his promise to Parliament and gave all the private assurances the French required. In December the English courts were forbidden to enforce the laws

James was a king who died six years too late. The verdict that posterity passed upon him would have been much more favorable had he been carried off during one of his gallstone attacks in 1619, before the great crises of his reign, those of the Palatinate and Spanish match.

—G. P. V. AKRIGG
Canadian historian

against Catholics, and Catholic prisoners were released.

The government had passed out of James's incapable hands. All he had now was his boys, and he feared irrationally that they would abandon him. The Spanish ambassadors told him Buckingham was a traitor and made him cry. The feeble 59-year-old king wrote his 32-year-old favorite a typically frank and touching letter in December 1624: "I pray God that I may have a joyful and comfortable meeting with you, and that we may make at this Christenmass a new marriage, ever to be kept hereafter. . . ."

There was time for one more calamity. A pitiful English army of 12,000 men, led by the cruel and incompetent mercenary Count Mansfeld, sailed off to fight for the Palatinate at the end of January 1625. Three-quarters of these warriors were dead of starvation, exposure, and disease before the end of March, without ever having struck a blow for Frederick.

On March 27, 1625, the first king of Great Britain, having suffered chills and fever, a stroke, paralysis, choking phlegm, and severe dysentery, died a miser-

James I of Great Britain died on March 27, 1625, after a debilitating illness. The remedies that had been sent to the king by Buckingham's mother caused rumors to spread that the favorite's family had poisoned the king.

William Shakespeare's numerous tragedies and comedies became famous under James I. *Macbeth* **and** *King Lear* **were performed for the king.**

able death. The elaborate and somewhat disorderly funeral was a fitting farewell to this disorderly, extravagant king: It was said to have cost around 50,000 pounds, a sum King Charles could ill afford.

James I of Great Britain was a man of wit and learning, of generosity and moderation and peace. His legacy includes his books and tender letters and, of course, the simple, beautiful King James Version of the Bible. Jacobean drama owes a great debt to the king, who was a strong patron of theater and literature. He gave support to Shakespeare's drama company, and it was during his reign that *Othello*, *King Lear*, and *Macbeth* were written. In fact, *Othello* and *King Lear* were performed at Whitehall before the king.

The erudite James was equally interested in promoting education. He signed the founding charter of the University of Edinburgh in 1582, made visits to both Oxford and Cambridge universities, and provided funding and lands for Trinity College in Dublin, Ireland. In 1621 James appointed John Donne, one of the greatest of the English poets, to be dean of St. Paul's Cathedral. Donne, an Anglican priest, presided over St. Paul's until his death in 1631 and is recognized today for his passionate and powerful love songs and religious verse.

It is the paradox of James's life that he craved power in a country whose traditions were alien to him and whose people he never truly understood. In 17th-century England the king's role in government was undergoing a radical redefinition. James's failures — his weakness, his rigid defense of absolute monarchy, his unnecessary conflicts with the Puritans and Parliament, his inefficiency, incompetence, and frequent lack of interest in running the government — did much to spur the development of traditions and institutions of representative democracy in England. A greater king might have inhibited those impulses and deflected those energies. In spite of himself, James helped plant the seeds that would bear such bitter fruit — for Buckingham, who was struck down by a pro-Parliament assassin in 1628; for Charles, who

Charles I was crowned king of England on March 27, 1625. He inherited his father's debt, a war with Spain, and an intensifying quarrel with an ever stronger Parliament. Charles suffered the consequences of James's inability to compromise with Parliament when he was deposed and executed in 1649.

would continue to assert the royal prerogative until Parliament deposed and beheaded him in 1649; and for England, which would fight a bloody and destructive civil war brought on by the struggle for power between king and Parliament. It was a haunting legacy for a king who hated bloodshed and wanted only peace.

Further Reading

Akrigg, G. P. V. *Jacobean Pageant*. Cambridge, MA: Harvard University Press, 1962.

Davies, Godfrey. *The Early Stuarts: 1603-1660*. Oxford: Oxford University Press, 1952.

Fraser, Antonia. *King James*. New York: Knopf, 1974.

Kenyon, J.P. *Stuart England*. New York: Penguin, 1980.

McElwee, William. *The Wisest Fool in Christendom*. New York: Harcourt, Brace and Co., 1958.

Scott, Otto J. *James I*. New York: Mason/Charter, 1976.

Willson, David Harris. *King James VI and I*. New York: Oxford University Press, 1967.

Chronology

June 19, 1566	James Stuart born at Edinburgh to Mary, queen of Scots and Henry, Lord Darnley
July 24, 1567	Mary forced to abdicate by Protestant nobles
July 29, 1567	James crowned as James VI of Scotland
Aug. 21, 1582	Kidnapped by Protestant lords in the Raid of Ruthven; escapes following June
Feb. 8, 1587	Mary is executed in England for treason
Aug. 28, 1589	James marries Anne of Denmark by proxy
Nov. 14, 1600	Prince Charles born at Dunfermline
March 24, 1603	Queen Elizabeth dies; James proclaimed King James I of Britain
Jan. 1604	James alienates Puritans at Hampton Court Conference
Aug. 1604	Concludes peace treaty with Spain
Nov. 1605	Catholics make assassination attempt on James in the Gunpowder Plot
Nov. 1610	The Great Contract is shelved due to bitter debates between Parliament and James
1611	James dissolves Parliament
	Rise to power of duke of Somerset
Feb. 14, 1613	Princess Elizabeth marries Frederick V, elector of the Palatinate
April 1614	"Addled Parliament" meets for two months
May 1616	Trial of Somerset exposes corruption in James's court; rise to power of duke of Buckingham
May 1617	James begins five-month progress in Scotland
May 1618	Defenestration of Prague signals outbreak of Thirty Years' War
Oct. 29, 1618	Sir Walter Raleigh is executed
Nov. 1620	Battle of the White Mountain; Frederick and Elizabeth flee Bohemia; James promises aid
Dec. 18, 1621	"Protestation" of Parliament challenges royal prerogative
Feb.–Oct. 1623	Prince Charles and Buckingham attempt to arrange Spanish match; James forced to agree to unacceptable terms to gain their release from Spain
March 27, 1625	James dies in London

Index

Frank Dwyer received his B.A. from New York University and his M.A. in English literature from the State University of New York at Buffalo, where he has also taught. A trained actor, he has directed or performed in numerous New York theater productions. His criticism, reviews, and poems have appeared in *Salmagundi*, *American Poetry Review*, and *Ploughshares*, among other publications. He is also the author of *Henry VIII* in the Chelsea House series WORLD LEADERS—PAST & PRESENT.

Arthur M. Schlesinger, jr., taught history at Harvard for many years and is currently Albert Schweitzer Professor of the Humanities at City University of New York. He is the author of numerous highly praised works in American history and has twice been awarded the Pulitzer Prize. He served in the White House as special assistant to Presidents Kennedy and Johnson.
